The Cure to Laziness (This Could Change Your Life)

Develop Daily Self-Discipline and Highly Effective Long-Term Atomic Habits to Achieve Your Goals for Entrepreneurs, Weight Loss, and Success

Stephen Martin

Contents

THE CURE

TO LAZINESS

THIS COULD CHANGE YOUR LIFE

DEVELOP DAILY SELF-DISCIPLINE AND HIGHLY EFFECTIVE
LONG-TERM ATOMIC HABITS TO ACHIEVE YOUR GOALS
FOR ENTREPRENEURS, WEIGHT LOSS, AND SUCCESS

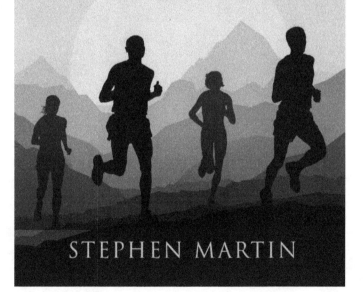

STEPHEN MARTIN

Introduction

"My will shall shape my future. Whether I fail or succeed shall be no man's doing but my own. I am the force; I can clear any obstacle before me, or I can be lost in the maze. My choice; my responsibility; win or lose, only I hold the key to my destiny." - Elaine Maxwell

When you take a general look at life, you will discover that it is full of people in various categories of success. Some people tend to enjoy the good things in life. Everything seems to work in their favor, and they live a happy, contented and prosperous life.

Many people start out at a tender age full of potentials, great hopes and aspirations for the future. However, just a few, just a handful of these people can achieve their goal, get a hold of their relationship and succeed in their business and career.

Of the many things that separate the successful class from the unsuccessful ones, self-discipline is a major key. No one plans to fail. As it's often said, success has many children, or should I say family relations. However, how many people are willing to give success what it takes?

We all desire to live the life of our dreams. Marry the girl of our dreams, go for vacation in Hawaii, live a life free from disease of all sorts, be able to buy whatever we need anytime, achieve financial success and be a responsible parent to our kids and a better partner to our spouse. The sad reality, however, is that not everyone is willing to give what it takes to achieve this.

We all know that success doesn't come on a silver platter. Deep down us all, we all know what we must do to make our goals and dream a success, a reality. As an obese person, I know what I must do to lose weight. A student knows what to do to increase the grade and be more successful. A wife/husband knows how they can make their family better and be a better partner for their better half. An addict is very much aware of the steps to break out of the addiction.

Intuitively, we all know what we must do in achieving our goals and making our life better. This is where the problems lie. Are we willing to give what it takes?

For whatever reason, we lack the willpower and discipline to really work towards achieving our goals. Many are less motivated, fond of procrastination, and can't just seem to get the push to strive at whatever it is they set their heart to achieve. Many are fond of making excuses for not getting started. This is where the power of self-discipline comes in.

How beautiful it is to desire to lose weight, set your heart at it and give it all it takes. What a wonderful thing it would be as a student to give it your all to get good grades in college! Committing to that exercise regimen is hard but imagine the wonders it will do to your body and overall health if you could just commit to it!

With the right training and mindset, you can set your heart to achieve anything it wants to achieve. You can train yourself to be strong, develop the right mindset, that of a Navy seal such that when you commit your heart to anything, you become like the wind, clearing away any obstacle standing as a hindrance.

One thing you should know and bear in mind is that people who are successful today are highly disciplined. Besides this, they developed this habit carefully through the mental workout and the right attitude. Imagine a gold medalist in the Olympics for instance. He doesn't just get all good overnight.

Through striving and toiling, through the right power, through discipline and courage, he trains himself. He subjects himself to harsh treatment all in the name of being ahead in the competition. With discipline, he motivates himself, trains himself, and gradually graduates from an amateur to a pro. With time, with self-discipline and resilience as an ingredient, he gradually becomes a professional when the training becomes part of him.

In other words, discipline is a habit that can be learned and developed. You can train it into your life. And if you have picked up this book, you have a very powerful resource in your hand to help you. You are just a step away from achieving whatever it is you set yourself to achieve.

This book will equip and instill in you the practical tool to achieve whatever it is you set your heart to. With the teachings here, you will understand that you can achieve anything. The human mind and will are powerful. With the right motivation and recipe (self-discipline as an ingredient here), it can achieve anything.

Success will no longer be alien to you since your will, coupled with self-discipline, can get you whatever you set your heart on. Then you now realize that successful people, people you count as extraordinary were ordinary men who have mastered the art of self-discipline and habits to achieve their goals.

You are in for a good read my friend. The fact that you chose to read this book rather than go out for a drink with your friends or watch a series on Netflix is an indication that you are just a step away from achieving self-discipline.

Bear in mind that the journey to self-discipline is not an easy one. It is often a lonely road full of temptations and resistance. But one thing

The Cure to Laziness (This Could Change Your Life)

I want you to remember is that you can do it. Set your mind on the goal. Imagine how beautiful and better off your life will be if you persevere and endure to the end. The right attitude and self-discipline, you will be able to surmount all obstacles on your path to realizing your dream.

On a final note, don't be like Jessica who frowns every time her husband drags her away from the bed to go for a jog. Neither be like Tom who feels his parents are punishing him since they seized his Xbox and PlayStation. My point is discipline is not a tool to make your life uncomfortable or necessary unbearable. While I admit that the journey to developing self-discipline is not an easy one, it is worth it. See the journey as a process, a step that will transform you into a better person, a personality you will be proud of.

As you journey through the pages of this book, keep in mind that with self-discipline and the right mindset, you can achieve whatever you set out to!

Chapter 1:
Self-Discipline

"We don't have to be smarter than the rest; we have to be more disciplined than the rest." -Warren Buffett

Self-discipline is one vital skill for success. Additionally, it is so important that the few people that strive to develop this virtue and strengthen it get to reap its benefit in all areas of their life.

Self-discipline simply means the ability to do what is expected of you. It involves doing away with instant gratification or present comfort for the purpose of long-term goals. This explains why Tom's parents had to seize his Xbox to enable him to study hard to get a good grade. Human beings are naturally drawn to entertainment. Hence, Tom's ability to see things from his parents' angle and understand that doing away with present comfort (staying away from Xbox and studying) will be of tremendous benefits for him in the future (good grades).

The fact is, as explained in the introduction, we all know what we need to do to make our life better. However, we lack the self-discipline and zeal to make this happen. It is self-discipline that gives the needed push to overcome the mental and physical barrier to move ahead with what we must do.

In contrary to how many people view self-discipline, it is neither being unreasonably hard/harsh towards yourself nor living a life devoid of fun and interesting things. Rather, self-discipline is one of the indications of inner strength, a form of self-control which enables you to take control of your life, your actions and reactions, and act based on reason and judgment.

Self-discipline gives you the mental toughness to decide and follow through, irrespective of the distractions and inconveniences to deviate. With this, self-discipline is a critical ingredient needed in seeing a goal or vision to reality.

When you have self-discipline, you will be able to stick to your goals and plans and see them through to manifestations. Self-discipline comes in various forms and can be said to be an inner strength giving you the needed boost to kickstart any plan, overcome the initial inertia, stop making excuses, do away with procrastination and follow through what you have got do.

Why Do You Need Self-Discipline?

Take a critical study of successful people in ministry, entertainment, business, and various career fields like celebrities, athletes, footballers, etc. One thing that makes successful ones stand out is the ability to stay focus and extremely disciplined in whatever they set their hearts to.

Hence, while success has many ingredients, self-discipline is like the core ingredient that binds every other part of the recipe. It is a vital habit that can be built over time via conscious and constant effort. It is a habit that many successful people have in common as they have developed and built this into their lives and characters over the years.

I will be sharing personal tips that worked for me, with which I became highly disciplined in life. I am not just sharing some theories or facts here. Rather, inscribed in the pages of this manual are techniques that have been applied to alter my path and take control of my life, career, and relationship for good.

Some years back, I lived a messed-up life and self-discipline was completely alien to me. I carried a lot of aggression and hatred around, especially when I lost my relationship of over five years. A relationship where I devoted my all. The breakup made me very violent and jealous of people with successful relationships. I lost the motivation to do anything tangible in life, and procrastination became the order of the day. I have experienced depression firsthand and never really had anything worthy to live for.

You can imagine how deep I was down the rabbit hole. However, somehow, I managed to get out of this state. This was years back. My transformation was not miraculous, as I took a conscious step to change the course of my life. This was what gave me the motivation to write this book. We as humans learn better through actions, hence, when you read the steps that helped transitioned my life, you will be able to relate. You will live a pretty content life and eventually get the freedom to dictate the course of your life, rather than living life base on impulse.

I have realized that self-discipline is the ability to control your basic desires that stem from pleasure. There are some negative habits that are inherent which many are fond of. Some examples are consuming excess sugar, not going for a workout, hitting the snooze button, avoiding new things, etc. These are negative habits that form the basic desires of man. Hence, an undisciplined man will rather listen to the dictates of his body, take the easy way out and do all the things listed above. However, if you are reading this book, there is a big chance, you are not part of the class described. I believe the desire to pick up this manual and read is the first step in building your self-discipline. You have been able to rise above the limitation and controls of your mind that probably wanted to do other less demanding things. This is one issue of average people who lack self-discipline. They follow the dictate of their mind like a zombie. The willpower and discipline to have a course and stay true to it are absent. This explains why procrastination forms the basis of their life. They are afraid to attempt anything new and they find it easier and preferable to curl up on the sofa and enjoy a movie rather than take up a task that will build up their mind and life in general.

Humans, generally, at any point in time, is about the body-mind connection. It is the mind that dictates to you. It forces you to do that task another time because you are not feeling like it. It tells you to hit the snooze button for ten more minutes of sleep. When you, however, get a grip on how to put your mind under total subjection, you can confidently say you own your self-discipline!

This explains why one of the major features of self-discipline is the ability to do away with instant gratification and pleasure, in expectation of a future, and much greater gain. This does not come easily, I will admit. Ask many people who have mastered the act of waking up early, I am pretty sure they will affirm that it was not easy at first. Besides, human generally is prone to favor and consider pleasures and things that will not stress them. This is the reason why it is easy to watch a series in one of your home videos, rather than launch your Kindle app and read a book that will make you better off! Self-discipline expresses itself in many ways:

- Perseverance – the ability to keep pushing despite setbacks and obstacles

- Self-Control – the ability to be focused in the face of temptation and distractions

- Resilience – being consistent with a task until you see it through to success

The journey to success is not an easy one. It is laden with distractions, challenges, obstacles, difficulties, and regrets. Yet, if you are going to be successful, you must be willing to rise above these which require self-control, perseverance and persistence, and above all, self-discipline.

When you develop these, you will lead a happy and fulfilled life, with the confidence that you can rise to achieve anything you set your heart to. How awesome is that!

With self-discipline, you get a hold of your life, be in charge and at the driver's seat of your life rather than following the dictates of your mind like a zombie. You live healthily; you accomplish your goals and set yourself up for spiritual improvement and growth.

Self-discipline is very important, and many people are aware of the importance and what you stand to gain from practicing self-discipline. However, only a few are willing to take the steps to develop, train and build their self-discipline. By picking up this book, I bet you are among the few. The pages of this book will equip you with all you need to know.

Benefits and Importance of Self-Discipline

If you were to seek advice from ten successful people, I am pretty sure eight of them will recommend self-discipline at its peak. It is not surprising as self-discipline plays a vital role in the recipe for success. However, what makes self-discipline so important?

- How do you become better off with self-discipline?

- Why is self-discipline vital in every aspect of human life?

Self-Discipline Helps You Feel Healthy

Excessive feeding, junk and fast foods, alcohol, etc. are not good for the health. There are many people out there that are controlled by their impulse to eat and drink. They lack control over their feeding habit when self-discipline is absent. When the inner strength to take charge of their feeding habit is absent, they just cannot seem to control it. Many people are fond of emotional eating – eating when angry, sad, or bored.

With discipline, however, people will stay away from junks, too much pizza, and fat-laden foods. With this, they can save themselves from various diseases that come from excessive sugar.

While many people are completely fine with a cup or two of alcohol, it becomes a problem for others who have turned it into a habit. It is when you are much disciplined that you can resist the urge to open another bottle of alcohol.

A person who drinks excessively hardly shows self-discipline. Therefore, they usually require help in terms of sobriety. And for sobriety to be genuinely effective, a very high degree of self-discipline is vital.

Self-Discipline Helps Form A Habit

Habits are the characters and traits you are known for. Habits are formed with time which can be maintained and solidified via self-discipline. Laziness is a form of habit peculiar to many people. This works against many people's effort to be disciplined.

Being able to wake up as early as 5:00 am is a habit that is already part of many people. This doesn't come naturally; it was developed over time through determination to resist the temptation of hitting the snooze button. And with time, the internal clock of this set of people became aligned with their alarm clock. Hence, once it is 5 am, they wake up.

Self-discipline will make you commit to something, set at it, and give it all it takes to see this to fruition.

Self-Discipline Is Important to Getting Things Done

It is when you have self-discipline that you get to resist procrastination and other distractions. These are the menace that could be vying for your attention at the expense of what you really must do. Self-discipline makes the difference between a student who would read his notebook and the other one who prefers to spend the day with Xbox.

Self-discipline is the basic ingredient you need to set your heart at something and complete it. With this type of character, it gradually becomes your personality, which sets you apart as an achiever in life.

It is the singular habit of self-discipline that makes you a tough personality that never gives up. Since self-discipline has resilience as one of its traits, nothing can stop you hence, you become a rigid and strong personality that is unstoppable.

Self-Discipline Helps You Commit to Exercise and Weight Loss

Many people see physical activities as stress. Yet, medical practitioners made us realize that there are tremendous benefits that come with leading an active lifestyle. Many people will rather curl up on the couch and watch an episode on Netflix, rather than go for a jog. Many will keep telling themselves they will go for that run the coming week, which never happens.

Exercise is however so vital that it can prevent the onset of many diseases in the body. Yet, it doesn't come naturally. It takes self-discipline to pay a gym membership fee and commit yourself to a regular visit. Even if you can't pay for gym membership, going for a walk, an early morning run or jog or any form of exercise all requires discipline.

Exercising your body is vital to your health which helps you lose weight. It is self-discipline that makes you resist distractions and procrastination. With self-discipline comes the inner strength and willpower to decide to exercise your body and commit to it.

Weight loss is not an easy process. It never comes on a platter of gold. It is a step by step process that requires a commitment to something (whether intermittent fasting, constant workout or diet plan) in a bid to get rid of excess fat.

If you want to try to lose weight via intermittent fasting, for instance, you need to religiously schedule you're eating period to a specific window. It takes self-discipline to commit to that. It takes self-discipline to resist the hunger pangs and commit to your endeavor to stay without food for the purpose of losing weight.

If you try to lose weight with a diet plan, it takes self-discipline to commit yourself to follow the meal plan. This involves doing away with junks and many foods that your taste bud finds pleasure in. This cannot happen without self-discipline. This explains why many people don't find success with their diet plan. They commit to it for a week or two and fail.

Self-Discipline Helps You Focus

There are many, many things in this present world that can distract you from your goal. Social media, entertainment, friends, etc., are the common source of distraction that prevents most. With self-discipline, however, you stay faithful and committed to your goal to be successful.

Being focused on your goal ensures you mark off every checklist item that is essential. There are many ingredients crucial for success. Self-discipline is one of the main recipes which also manifest itself as a focus.

To a person that wants to lose weight, for instance, she could have the picture of a model hung up in her bedroom. Every morning, she sees the picture, reminding herself of her goal. This keeps her focused, giving her the motivation to do all she has to do to achieve her goal.

Self-Discipline Brings Out the Best in You

Success never comes on a platter of gold, neither does it goes to the slothful. Every day, if you desire to be successful, you must keep striving to bring out the best in you. An athlete, for instance, needs to practice daily and strive to improve on his previous day performance.

This only happens with self-discipline. It is that ingredient that can keep you on track and help you commit to doing what needs to be done to achieve success.

On the race to success, self-discipline is one of the most important factors that will keep you on track. Without this, there is a high tendency that people with more discipline will knock you out of the race.

Chapter 2:
Build Self-Discipline

Self-discipline is an important ability you must build to gain the best experiences in life. People often feel apprehensive when they hear the term "Discipline" because it is associated with being confined or fixated on a specific routine that makes them feel like they have lost all access to freedom. This popular notion of discipline is far from the truth, and you are about to discover the power that lies within being a self-disciplined individual.

You can't speak about developing willpower and control over your life without first dealing with the concept of discipline. Self-discipline is the capacity you build to control yourself and to make yourself behave in a certain way without needing anybody to tell you what to do. It is also one of the most useful skills you will need in every area of life.

When a person is said to be self-disciplined, it means he/she has gained inner strength and the power to make decisions without being conflicted. This assertion implies that there is a connection between being disciplined and building willpower (We will deliberate more about this in the next chapter). Think about this for a moment, when was the last time you decided on something and stuck to it till you accomplished it? Do you remember having to create a daily plan and being disciplined enough to see it come to fruition? Have you ever fulfilled an obligation or kept a promise despite stiff oppositions?

If you think back to all the experiences you've had, you will agree that there were times when you wanted to do all you set out to accomplish but fell short of expectations. You didn't fail at such instances, come on, you did well for even trying, but if you had built self-discipline, the chances of succeeding would have been higher.

So, you see, being self-disciplined doesn't mean you get to be so hard on yourself. It merely gives an opportunity to stick to the positive changes, decisions, ideas and action plan you require for a fantastic life. Everyone is at a different level with being self-disciplined, we all have our triumphant moments and our "Keep on trying" moments, but regardless of the level you currently are right now, you should know that the journey to being self-disciplined is a continuous one.

When you decide to be self-disciplined, most of the time, circumstances and situations seem to arise that make it difficult for you to stick to your plan. Now in those moments, it becomes effortless and convenient to let yourself go instead of being guided by discipline.

This situation is a challenge millions of people face all over the world but guess what? There are ways of ensuring that you stick to your plans, read to discover the answers. Self-discipline is not gained when you say, "I want to be a disciplined person", it is also not built when you imitate someone you think is disciplined, neither does it become a reality when you become disciplined for a week after reading this book. Self-discipline can be attained through your habits!

How to Form A Habit?

Habits, yes, those activities you do every day without fail consciously or unconsciously can make or break your journey to be a self-disciplined individual. Your ability to build and sustain the right habits goes a long way in helping you attain the goals and expectations you have for your life.

There are several ways of ensuring you cultivate productive habits, but the most effective step is having a programmed behavioral pattern. The concept of a programmed behavior refers to the way a person builds up his/her resistance level to certain things that hinders the sustainability of a good habit. Experts on this subject suggest that if your habits prevent you from being self-disciplined, you must develop new ones, but there is a caveat.

Developing new patterns is not the problem, breaking away from the old ones is where the challenge lies and until you handle this issue, you will never attain the level of self-discipline you desire.

So, we are back to the most viable solution you can implement which entails developing a programmed behavior. Here's a scenario, you know the importance of reading, as such you resolve to read more books this year. For you to accomplish this goal, it is essential that you stop attending parties on weeknights. Now, this friend of yours invites you over for a party just as you are about to start reading a book; suddenly you feel tempted to attend one last party after all, one party wouldn't hurt.

You put your shoes on, have a great time at the event but it will be harder for you to say "No" the next time you are invited. Gradually, you forget about the commitment you made to reading and go back to the partying habits which contribute to a lack of self-discipline in your life.

However, if you had a programmed behavior, you will be able to resist the temptations and stick to your new habits, so what is it exactly? A programmed behavior means being intentional with your habits; it is a manner of conducting yourself in such a way that you are 100% committed to your new traditions.

There are two phases to building a programmed behavior; the first stage requires the individual getting rid of the bad habit and the second stage entails replacing that bad habit with a good pattern.

Once you get both phases set up, you must ensure that you stick to them regardless of the enticement. A person who has adopted a programmed behavior will decline the invitation to a party and immediately start reading, shutting out every other consideration that will lead to a change of plans. This is how you build self-discipline with your habits; by being deliberate with the decisions you take.

It takes a while to form a new habit, but you can get ahead of time by starting and repeating the new habit daily until you succeed. The first few days of implementation might seem like a daunting challenge, but if you persist, you will become more comfortable with time.

When you think about a programmed character, cast your mind back to an automated machine; such a device will only render products and services it is programmed to give. The same applies to you; a programmed mindset can only allow what the new habits entail so not giving in to the wrong habits become natural to you.

Programmed behavior also helps you remain constantly reminded of your goals; you become fixated on what you want to accomplish that you don't give room for anything less. This approach to self-discipline works with any goal you set for yourself: weight loss, career goals, etc. First, program your mind to resist wrong and stick to good then you will be on your way to becoming a self-disciplined person.

Exercise is an activity that can help you build a programmed behavior. If you are a fitness enthusiast, you will agree that the process of keeping fit is one that demands some programming of the mind. Fitness practices must be done according to the dictates of time and effort; to achieve certain milestones, you must be doing or must have done some severe activities.

If you want to become a very self-disciplined person using the principle of programmed behavior, you may have to start taking exercises seriously. The connection between exercises, habits and self-disciplined lies in the fact that with exercises there are a lot of routines, sets and timings one must rely on. A person struggling with sustaining a new habit will find it easier to do so if he/she starts taking exercise seriously.

So, the same determination used to attain a 10,000-step walk can be used to say "No" when necessary and stick to the newly formed habit. Exercise is also a positive habit that leads to the development of other outstanding traditions such as resting, drinking more water, and engaging in healthier activities that inspire you to maintain good habits.

As you create and maintain an exercise schedule, you will also be doing the same with your new patterns, and this is all because you decided to have a programmed behavior towards life. As you work on implementing a programmed behavior, you shouldn't miss out on building a new personality. Old habits have a way of affecting our characters; you do something for so long until it becomes a part of you.

So, try positive things today, set the old ways aside by being committed to a sustainable process which guarantees self-discipline. Discipline is all about control; it is about your ability to take charge of your life and determine what is right for you while sticking to it. Why will anyone want to exercise control? Why can't we live the way we want to? Why are you reading this book learning about how to be self-disciplined? There are so many "Why's" to answer, and until you provide answers, you will not get the best out of this experience.

Determine Your Why

Getting to know the reason for attaining self-discipline will give you an encouraging boost that will cause you to be more focused on your long-term goals as opposed to being concerned about immediate fulfillment. You can know why you are doing this through goals; your goals must be powerful enough to set you sailing on the right course and help you resist the temptation of going back to bad habits that stifle you.

A lot of times when individuals set goals, they try to attain the goals and hope that the process will help them become better with being disciplined. However, when they observe that they are still not as disciplined as they want to be, they become frustrated with the effort and quickly give up. The problem isn't with goal setting; it is with the quality of goals you set. You must have explicit goals; this refers to targets that are detailed enough to provoke an essential response from you. Shall we relate to the scenario used when discussing habits?

Setting a goal to read more books in a year isn't powerful enough as such when your friend sends an invitation for a party on a weeknight, you will oblige because you didn't give your goals enough details. On the other hand, if you had explicitly mentioned that your aspiration to read two books per month and a total of 24 books in a year, you will have created a compelling goal.

Now, having this exact intention in mind will cause you to decline the invitation because at that time, you are probably still on one book and it is already the second week of the month. When you have a specific goal, it causes you to think about the long-term result that goal will fetch you and all these considerations will make it possible for you to stay focused on attaining the vision thus fighting off the temptation that makes you undisciplined. Simply put, make your goals come alive with facts!

The next step you should take after setting goals is to utilize the power of imagination. Now that you are armed with the right aspirations, it is crucial that you start thinking about the results even now.

What do you want to achieve with these goals? How will you feel when you eventually smash the objectives and win? Time spent thinking about the possible outcomes of your goals is instrumental in helping you stay motivated enough to accomplish your set targets. So, there you are, visualizing how you will be after hitting your target of 24 books in a year, think of how much knowledge you will acquire that will be contributory in helping you grow career-wise.

Envisaging your goal is a good step but there is something even better than that, and it is being focused on the progression you make towards the goal. If you have taken the time to create a goal that helps you read two books every month, you should be concerned about how you are going to achieve this.

To become a self-disciplined person, you must be committed to the realization of the process as much as you are committed to fulfilling the goal. People are always so fixated on the goal, wanting to attain a certain height but they forget that there is a process to follow as such if the process isn't right, the target will not be achieved.

You've got to train your mind to create a method that will be effective in attaining your goals. Using the situation, we've been working with, this means that you must be willing to create a "Reading plan" that suits your schedule and enables you to read the set number of books in that month. If you stay focused on this process long enough, if you are consumed with the idea of doing it, you will achieve your long-term goals.

Now that you can create the right habits and be more specific with your goals, you are closer to establishing the pathway to being self-disciplined. If you are wondering if there is still one more stop to make, you are right, we must talk about the concept of being absorbed with original ideas.

Focus on Essential Tasks

Being self-disciplined is not about being frustrated and forced to do the things you don't like just because you want to attain specific goals. On the contrary, it is possible to be a disciplined person who still loves whatever he/she does. If you are going to develop and build up a new habit, it should be something you do because you will enjoy it as opposed to doing it because everyone else requires it of you.

This means that if you must engage in exercises for the sake of your health and someone suggests walking around the neighborhood, you can decline if that form of exercise isn't fun for you. You can try swimming, jogging, weightlifting or something else that will help you exercise and still achieve your goals; this is how you concentrate on the basic ideas.

In a bid to do it all, some people end up feeling flustered, unhappy and depressed about not being self-disciplined. The problem can be traced to the fact that they are doing all these activities to impress others and until they start to focus on fundamentals, they will continue to struggle.

This is a vital lesson you must instill: don't try to accomplish so many tasks at once. Yes, you've got the passion for doing more, and you are ready to take up the challenge, but would it be better if you tried to do these numerous things and felt overwhelmed or would you prefer to do what you genuinely enjoy?

If your affirmative answer is to the latter question, then you must set goals and form new habits that fit into the plan you've got for your life. Take on the reading challenge because you love books, not because you feel compelled to do it.

As you redirect your energies towards things that excite you, there will be a significant change with the level of discipline you enjoy, and this will also help you have a firmer grip on your goals.

To summarize the notion of being absorbed with basic ideas, you should do what you love and not what you are expected to do. Enjoy the tasks that are best suited for your life and bask in the feel of being able to live freely. If you are going to be self-disciplined, you shouldn't engage in tasks you find unnecessary; redirect your energies to things you can do joyfully while maintaining your stance.

Mostly, you should do the things you believe will work for you; the importance of this aspect cannot be overemphasized because there are too many people who misunderstand the message of discipline. Such persons become so stiff with life, living every day doing what they think they "Should" do as opposed to doing what they "Love" to do. For a fact, you will become more disciplined when you are living on your own terms because you are not pressured by any task or forced to do something you are not comfortable with.

By being selective with what you choose to do, you empower yourself to live by your own rules which is instrumental in increasing your level of discipline. Taking on more than what you can handle is a sign of being undisciplined and the only way to rectify this is by sticking to the principle of selectivity. Be careful with what you decide to take on; all your decisions, habits and goals should be motivated by what you enjoy.

The journey to becoming a self-disciplined person is an enduring one, but you have taken the first step which is quite commendable. You must continue to mold yourself daily with real concepts and action plans that give you the desired results. In the next chapter we continue our discourse on self-discipline from a refreshing perspective, do enjoy the read.

Chapter 3:
The Truth: Self-Discipline Vs Willpower

"Willpower is what separates us from the animals. It's the capacity to restrain our impulses, resist temptation – do what's right and good for us in the long run, not what we want to do right now. It's central, in fact, to civilization." -Dr. Roy Baumeister, Ph.D.

If you want to achieve anything significant in life you must be self-disciplined; this is a fundamental truth to embrace first before any-thing else. When a person starts to feel like he/she has achieved less of the kind of success that was anticipated, the problem can be traced to the absence of discipline.

There is also the concept of willpower which is gaining a lot of atten-tion these days with people who want to do better with their lives. But before we consider the idea behind willpower, you should know why it is an alternative tool for self-discipline.

When people struggle with any form of addiction or personal issue, they tend to try and muscle their way out of it by showing the power of their "Will" against that problem. But think about it this way, will there be a problem in the first place if they were disciplined?

Self-discipline Vs. Willpower underscores the importance of taking care of a potential problem even before it becomes an actual challenge. With the former idea, you are taking charge, not giving room for an issue.

While with the latter, you are trying to take on a full battle with the problem hoping that as you go "cold turkey" on it, there will be a difference. When you understand the differences between both ideals, you will become empowered to use them right.

There is a time when willpower becomes useful in life generally, but it can't be used to replace the importance of self-discipline. In this chapter, you are going to discover some striking similarities between self-discipline and willpower.

You will also become conversant with the reason why self-discipline trumps the idea of willpower when dealing with life's issues. Willpower has its advantages, but the major point is that it shouldn't be used as a substitute for self-discipline. So, what is willpower?

Willpower refers to the unwavering strength to perform one's wishes; it is also the ability to control one's impulses or actions. Considering willpower from the perspective of dealing with an issue, it is a concept that teaches you to use all your mental, emotional and physical strength to deal with the problem and win.

If you have been dealing with an addiction or exposure to bad habits with willpower, you will try to fight it off. When you eventually win, you will feel good for a moment, but you might become vulnerable to a relapse.

With self-discipline, you train your mind, body, and soul to resist the issues you are dealing with, and this training is what helps you establish stability and consistent growth such that your success story becomes a source of encouragement to other people.

Self-Discipline: A Training Channel

When self-discipline is viewed as a training process, it starts to work for an individual. Do you remember when you were in school? How you needed the help of your tutor to understand some of the most complex topics taught?

Well, that tutor made it possible for you to develop a study pattern which became part of the reasons why you became successful in school. Every tutor sets the foundational idea on which the student's academic success is built upon.

However, your tutor couldn't have been with you all the time, he/she wouldn't write the examination for you as well so what do you do?

Firstly, you must understand that the tutor's role is consultative, a more significant percentage of the work to be done lies within you.

This is often the problem with people who struggle with self-discipline; they want the tutor with them all the time, they are not willing to do things on their own. A dietician must remind them to eat the right foods, a gym instructor must push them to exercise, and when these "Tutors" are not available, they fall like a pack of cards.

Self-discipline is a training channel that offers you a unique opportunity to do the things that are right by you without anyone compelling you to. When you start to imbibe the principles of being disciplined, you train yourself to identify the areas you should focus on while working towards being self-reliant (we will discuss on the concept of being self-reliant very soon).

You might need a tutor at the beginning of your journey (everyone needs a helping hand) but after the tutor gives you the necessary training, get on with the processes and protocols on your own. Train yourself daily to carry out those activities your tutor has taught you and gain mastery over them. Self-discipline doesn't mean you must deprive yourself of some things; it just says that you are willing to train yourself until you attain a level of expertise.

When you realize that you are training yourself for the future, you put your goals in focus and strive to attain them. So, at this point, you are not propelled by the desire to impress your tutor; instead, you are inspired by the image of success and fulfillment you visualize upon achieving your objectives.

The result of being self-disciplined is independence. You know you are closer to the goal of being self-disciplined when you start to do those positive things that transform your life for good.

Being Self-Reliant

While the training process to becoming self-disciplined doesn't end, it does contribute to making you an independent person. So back to the tutor story, as you listen and imbibe all the tutor teaches, you start to understand why being self-disciplined is essential.

Gradually, you begin to do those things that uplift you without seeking the guidance of your tutor. Now what happens to you is that you start to trust yourself again, you say to yourself "I can do this," and you watch those things come to life.

Being self-reliant is an aspect of self-discipline some people never attain because they don't have enough faith in themselves. They take one step out of that addiction problem today and take several steps backward. They try to drink more water for a week and become de-hydrated for another month.

Until there is a commitment to your progress, you will struggle with being over-reliant on your tutor. You've got to understand that while a tutor is a guide, you are the executor. No one will ever understand your desire to be better at what you do better than you, which is the reason why it is your responsibility to push yourself despite having a tutor.

You might want to ask, "How do I know when I become self-reliant?" Well, you will know that you have become independent when you carry out the activities that propel you to make progress WITHOUT anyone's nudging.

This means you wake up in the morning for that early run around the park if you have a fitness challenge. The wrong foods are thrown out of the refrigerator if you are dealing with a weight problem. You get to read more books if you want to attain more knowledge and you do all that is required of you on your own terms. When you start to do these things, you can tell that you are now a self-reliant person who can make progress without being told what to do.

Another way you can tell if you are becoming independent is when you find yourself motivating other people to attain their goals as well. They say the best way to become more is by giving more and you cannot inspire someone else if you still struggle with your reality.

The moment you start acting like a tutor to someone else who struggles with a similar challenge just like you, that is the moment when you have become the best version of yourself.

Self-discipline empowers you thus creating multiple avenues through which you can help someone else become better. You start to see yourself as a tutor as well. Being able to help someone else will solidify all you know and set you on the course to consistent success with whatever you are dealing with.

The fact that you become self-reliant doesn't mean you also become a perfectionist with discipline. There will be challenging times when it seems like you are not so confident. What can you do when faced with such a trial?

Failure Is Part of The Process

The fact that you recognize how powerful it is to be self-disciplined is commendable, but beyond that, you should prepare for the eventuality of making mistakes and learning from them. People get into trouble for relying on willpower alone. If you are going to focus on willpower as an alternative to self-discipline, you will not be able to handle mistakes when they happen. This is because willpower makes you believe that you can do it all.

With willpower there is no preparation for failure at any time during the process, so with you not being prepared for failure, you might give in to the problem when mistakes occur. Self-discipline prepares you for success and empowers you with the right mindset to handle errors. As it is with other training opportunities, you will become conversant with the steps you can take when there is an unexpected challenge.

So, being self-disciplined or having willpower doesn't exempt you from problems but self-discipline makes you develop a tough skin such that you can deal with those mistakes if they happen.

You may have had a plan to change your diet because you want to look trim and fit. Even after sticking to healthy meals for a while, you might experience a "Fall" someday which makes you eat potato chips forgetting that you are on a strict diet.

If you were focused on willpower, you would be devastated, thinking "What have I done?" "I thought I was strong enough to handle this," but if you were relying on the training you've got with discipline, you would realize that "Yes, I made a mistake, but I am not going back to it, neither will I let this error get the best of me."

Self-discipline doesn't make you feel less of yourself when you make a mistake; it's all a part of the training process. It's like being in school, you pass some tests excellently, and then you don't excel with others, but you keep pressing on knowing that both the good and the not so good ones contribute to giving you a fantastic experience.

Failure as a part of the process shouldn't give you the leeway to make mistakes intentionally. But it helps you become comfortable with the idea of failing that you are not frightened by it.

In the absence of the fear of failure, you will be confident enough to face your future with positive expectations. Once you deal with the challenge of fear, you can achieve a lot on this journey to self-discipline.

Learning Never Ends

One of the most fantastic feelings you enjoy when you are a self-disciplined individual is that you get to learn every day! Yes, there is a lesson for you to gain daily and it all contributes to making the process of being disciplined even easier.

As opposed to be a person who uses willpower and continually wants to rely on the ability of self, self-discipline allows you to learn from everything. You get to learn from your environment, the decisions you make and every other experience you create on this journey.

If you are self-disciplined, you will be self-conscious as well. There is an awareness you have that makes it possible for you to take note of everything you do. This means you get to learn more about what is right and what isn't right for you thus helping you make better choices.

If you are thinking about kicking out your addictions, you will have to be self-disciplined first; not just because you want to fight off the addiction but because you are willing to learn more about yourself.

Some therapists who try to help people out with challenges discover that when a person is self-disciplined, he/she tends to find new ways of tackling the problem on their own because we are programmed to learn lessons about ourselves when we are disciplined.

Think about this; the moments you lived without being conscious of discipline were probably the times when you felt like you couldn't handle the challenges you were faced with. This was also because you weren't aware of yourself nor your potentials.

Self-discipline makes it possible for you to always keep your life in perspective and this is a significant pathway to continuous learning. You become aware of your strengths and weaknesses while enjoying the former and working on the latter.

If you are currently struggling with something you want to change in your life; a habit, thought process or issue, focus on being self-disciplined and you will be able to solve the problems without getting help from a third party.

The principle of continuous learning by being self-disciplined helps an individual take responsibility for their actions. It is easy to blame someone else for our errors when we aren't disciplined enough to see where we falter.

The Cure to Laziness (This Could Change Your Life)

If you have ever disciplined a child before, you probably heard all sorts of excuses from the child "It wasn't my fault" "It was Dilly who tipped the cup over, I just watched it trip and spill."

As funny as these simple childish responses are, you get to see that the undisciplined child never takes responsibility and it is the same for adults. If you are going to be the best version of yourself by being disciplined, while learning consistently with a strength of character, you must be willing to take responsibility for your actions.

Remember that you are on a journey; you may wobble off the track at some point, but you can always return to the records and keep up. This is another reason why self-discipline is better than willpower.

The desire to become achievers is innate in everyone, from the time individuals start to learn about life till the day they die, there will always be a consistent quest for attainment, but only one thing is needful to make it happen; self-discipline.

This chapter has been all about juxtaposing two compelling concepts in a bid to show which one works best and how you can utilize it for your long-term plans. If you have been struggling with challenges, habits, and addictions, it is probably because you are using willpower.

Build up your character and increase your capacity to always do the right things by being self-disciplined. Think about being disciplined as the foundational ideal you must implement first before considering willpower. You will be motivated to put up a fight with whatever you want to change (willpower) after you have toughened yourself up with training that helps instill a sense of discipline in you.

You are still on this journey to being self-disciplined; there are so many instructions and ideas to grasp from other sections. While you anticipate the content of the chapters to come, get ready to gain access to useful starting tips that will help you overcome challenges with self-discipline every day.

Chapter 4:
Starting Tips for Self-Discipline

"It is our choices that show what we truly are, far more than our abilities." -J.K. Rowling

You now have an advanced understanding of what self-discipline is about, from basic concepts to comparisons to other similar ideas that form the foundational beliefs of the subject matter.

We have succeeded in creating a pattern of information that aids the process of self-discipline for you. It is essential that you always remind yourself of all you've discovered thus far because the ideas are in a sequence.

This chapter takes things up a notch by introducing some of the most useful tips you can imbibe before becoming a disciplined individual. When you get to the end of this chapter, you will start taking proactive measures towards bringing these tips to life through actionable plans.

The previous chapter espoused on the relationship between self-discipline and willpower, and facts which explained why you should be focused on developing the former.

However, in that detailed chapter, you weren't shown the tips to implement that will help you choose discipline over willpower, so the objective of this chapter is to teach you all about that and more.

You should note that these tips will be most effective when you stick to them for an extended period. The best way to achieve sustainable results is by incorporating solutions to daily routines.

The previous chapter elaborated on the idea of self-discipline being a training process; now you should hold that thought in mind as you read through because what you will discover in this chapter are the tools needed for the training.

Remove Temptations

Everyone who is trying to become better with self-discipline is trying to get over some challenge or personal problem that causes them a lot of discomforts. It might be dealing with procrastination, addictions, weight gain, lack of focus, or whatever troubles your mind.

The problem will not just go away because you want it to, neither is it going to dissipate because you suddenly realize the importance of self-discipline. You need to know that every issue a human being is faced with is triggered by certain factors.

The Cure to Laziness (This Could Change Your Life)

If you discover that you always go to work late despite having good intentions, don't try to wake up and go to work early the following day, you need first to discover why you have been going to work late all the time; this is how you take care of a problem from its roots.

When you get the reasons, you become aware of your temptations, and you've got to remove them immediately. Eliminating temptation means getting rid of the things that serve as distractions to you.

Whatever you do that makes you go back to the same habits or patterns that are not productive is a distraction, and until you figure out how to get rid of them for good, you will consistently struggle with the problem. So, you know what you are dealing with; it might even be something worse than being late to work, it might be a challenge no one knows you are dealing with. Well for you to cross over to the self-disciplined side, you need to detoxify your life.

Your desire to become a self-disciplined person will never be attained if you keep going back to feed what tempts you, even when you do it in secret. The temptation must go, and it does take an amount of discipline to do that.

If you want to be more productive at work, you must show up early enough to get started with the day's activities. Going to bed late the previous night is an example of temptation with the ripple effect. So, what do you do?

You must set up restrictive measures that make it possible for you to go to bed early so you can wake up on time the following day. One of such restrictive rules includes having dinner on time, turning off the tv before bedtime, and sleeping at a designated time every evening.

The fact that you set such restrictive measures doesn't mean the temptation goes away immediately. Your body will try to resist, but if you persist, you will get used to it. Addiction can also be very challenging especially when it's a secret, but you can get over that addiction and live freely. First, discover the temptations and cut them off.

As you set up those restrictive barriers, get an accountability partner who checks up on you and monitors your progress. An accountability partner can be a close friend who is very disciplined, your boss at the office (if it is a work-related challenge) or a third-party expert who can help you get back on track when you miss a step.

To become a self-disciplined person, you must be selective with everything you do; some activities will set you back, and others will inspire you to become better. Eliminate the distractions and temptations while focusing on definite ideas that bring you closer to the goal.

Watch What You Do
As you disregard the temptations and distractions, also remember to become conscious of when you feel hungry, angry, tired or lonely.

These are feelings that make you vulnerable and cause you to be un-disciplined.

So, you need to understand why you feel the way you do and then figure out a way to get out of it immediately. Watching what you do refers to being conscious of how your feelings drive you to action.

If you are trying to become healthier through the foods you eat, your body might not warm up to the fruits and veggies you feed it, so you are bound to feel "Hungry" at some point.

Now feeling hungry here means the desire for the kind of unhealthy foods you used to enjoy. Instead of you getting the potato chips, burgers and lots of carbs, try to decipher why you feel hungry and then eat more of the healthy stuff because that is what self-disciplined people do.

If you have had a sad upbringing with lots of family issues, you are bound to feel angry every day. Your anger wouldn't steam from what happens around you but comes from within you.

You should figure out what makes you angry and deal with it! Even if it is an event from the past, be courageous, forgive those who hurt you and move on in faith. You are on the road to becoming a self-disciplined individual, and this means you must become bold about reaching out to what makes you an even better person. If you are angry, try to be calm.

When a person is tired, he/she will most likely not make good decisions and this why when you feel tired - get some rest. It is okay to take a break from everything else that competes for your attention and relax.

For you to be self-disciplined, you should know when your body and mind needs to get detached. But if you continue to push yourself, you will start to feel agitated which gives room for you to make wrong decisions.

Are you dealing with the loss of a loved one? Have your friends deserted you or are you surrounded by a lot of people but still feel lonely? You cannot make progress with self-discipline feeling this way.

Loneliness makes a person feel like he/she doesn't have to be accountable to anyone else, so that gives room for bad decisions. Whenever you feel lonely, reach out to someone, if you are overwhelmed by trouble, get friends and family to help.

You are not an island, and everyone needs help at some point in their lives. Being self-disciplined means, you love who you are enough to make the right decisions for yourself, and if you fancy yourself, you will reach out to those who can help when you need it the most.

Always watch what you do; your actions are a product of your feelings so check on yourself often. How are you feeling now? Why do you think that way? What can be done to make it all better? Get answers and don't stay too vulnerable for long.

Don't wait for it to "Feel right."

Waiting for the feeling is like waiting for the good decisions you make to "Feel right," and if you continue to wait, you will be passing on a brilliant opportunity to become self-disciplined.

Now we need to get into the human brain for a few moments here; there are two parts of the brain, one aids your habits and the other your decisions. The role of your brain that focuses on decisions loves to stick to a routine.

That part of your brain is used to the predictable decisions you will take so there is often no room for changes or new choices. Now if you want to get better with being self-disciplined, you must make changes with everything that pertains to your life.

This means that when you do go ahead to make the changes, your brain tries to reject it, and this makes you feel uncomfortable. At this stage, you start to "Feel" like maybe you shouldn't implement the changes anymore, but you cannot afford to do so!

You shouldn't wait for the perfect sunny feeling that gives you an affirmative nudge, and whenever you feel like you shouldn't be doing something new, that is the right time to do it.

That feeling of being uncomfortable is what strengthens the new habit you are about to form. Your mind or your brain may not be prepared for the change, but for you to be self-disciplined, you need to shut down that feeling and stick to what you know is required.

If you have been struggling with a problem, a bad habit or an addiction, it is probably because your mind is trying to reject the new ideas you want to implement.

If you were born and raised in a city and lived there for a long time as an adult, you will find that you have become accustomed to the food, their way of life and tiny details that make the place home.

When you move away for a while even for a short vacation, you will not get used to the food and lifestyle of the new place overnight. The food might taste too spicy, the environment might feel cold and you start to feel like you should go home.

If you hold on for a few more days, you will get used to the new environment, but if you give up and go home, you will probably never get used to anywhere else, and that's just sad.

Your journey to being self-discipline is like the experience you have in a new place, if you wait until it all feels perfect, you will lose out on the experience entirely. For self-discipline to be possible, you must look beyond your feelings, else you will be ruled by them.

Schedule Breaks

While trying to be self-disciplined, it is possible to get carried away with the process and forget to take a break. You've come a long way, even with this book and you deserve a treat.

However, in a bid to give yourself a treat, you shouldn't go back to the habits you are trying to abstain from. Before you give yourself one, make sure you have done something worthy, like a milestone.

Planning breaks make it possible for you to appreciate how far you have come while anticipating more success. The idea behind self-discipline can be taken so seriously by some people that they are not willing to do anything else except being disciplined.

When you go a long way and do good to yourself by reaching your goals, take a breather and chill off the pressure. You are not supposed to be immensely consumed with the idea of being disciplined, else you will feel stressed.

So, what is that thing you've always wanted to buy for yourself? How about dinner at an excellent restaurant? You could go to the park and have a nice time with your kids (if you have any), ice cream, etc.

Taking a break helps you get an honest assessment of how far you have come with being disciplined and what more you can do to get better. But in that state of relaxation, your mind is also at peace, and you feel like you have broken even with the process.

If you have been trying to get over an addiction for a while, set a target for yourself entailing what you should do on a daily, weekly, monthly and yearly basis. When you hit your daily goal, give yourself a high-five or a pat on the back.

If you hit your weekly goals, oh that calls for some ice cream and a sweet little treat. With your monthly successes, you can get yourself a nice present and when you hit the significant annual milestone, do something nice for yourself (something you have never done before).

The rewards and treats will also serve as an encouraging factor for you on this journey to self-discipline. Thinking about what you will do for yourself when you reach a milestone will propel you always to do your best.

It's like a child who waits for the treats from Santa Claus every Christmas, the child becomes well-behaved to be on Santa's good books, and that is how this process will be for you.

Be intentional about taking breaks periodically, in fact; you should work towards the breaks such that when you are ready to celebrate, you have the right resources. More importantly, it takes a lot of discipline to hit a target so in a bid to reach that goal you set for yourself, you will take disciplined steps that take you closer to your goal. You will fight off the addiction, kick off that bad habit and recreate a new life for yourself.

Forgive Yourself

As mentioned in a previous chapter, becoming self-disciplined is a process that isn't entirely smooth. You will be putting your best foot forward but will be faced with stiff opposition especially if you have practiced that bad habit or addiction for a long time.

Regardless of how many times you experience a relapse, you must be willing to forgive yourself and move on. Yes, there are going to be some slip-offs, and you will feel disappointed in yourself especially if you had faith in your ability to handle the situation.

However, forgiveness should come naturally to you. Being hard on yourself for making mistakes isn't the right move. When you are open about your vulnerability, you become empowered to minimize errors.

So, assuming the errors do happen, what you should do is share your failings with someone you trust. If you have an accountability partner, he/she will be the best person to share your feelings with.

After sharing, forgive your errors and make a promise to yourself that you wouldn't fall short of expectations again. Now that you are on the pathway to self-discipline, it will inspire you to fulfill your promises and keep your word.

This tip is one of the reasons why you were admonished not to depend on willpower earlier. With willpower, you will want to lean on your ability and physical strength forgetting that these factors can be affected.

Don't rely on willpower, just be disciplined enough to acknowledge when you are wrong and live freely. Shame has a cruel way of taking over your freedom; it makes you feel like you haven't achieved anything so it shouldn't be encouraged.

First, be committed to the process, do your best, don't compromise on the standards and let the process be your focal point. When you do all these, you have ticked the relevant boxes, but did you know that people still failed in their attempt to become self-disciplined even after trying these?

So, doing everything by the books isn't a guarantee that you wouldn't experience some failings on your part. Just continue to do the right things, pick yourself up when you fall and keep your eyes on the goal.

You have a responsibility to encourage yourself every day; if you make a mistake, you can tell yourself, "Oh that was a bad day, but I will do better next time" these real push-ups make it possible for you to stay on course.

Don't hold a grudge against yourself and don't be angry at your shortcomings. Sometimes these errors in judgment help strengthen your resolve to become the most self-disciplined person who can hold his/her head high and still make a lot of personal impacts.

The Cure to Laziness (This Could Change Your Life)

We are always listening to messages and reading books that urge us to forgive others who err while showing kindness to people who make mistakes. But what about you? Who forgives you when you aren't at your best? So be kind to yourself as well; be patient with your process and have some faith in yourself.

While striving to become a self-disciplined person, learn to show some compassion to yourself. There will be days when you don't feel so confident but even on those days, continue to do your best.

Tips for self-discipline are motivating factors that can inspire you daily. It can be a fascinating time for you if you want to lose weight and get a "Bikini body," but it also means that you must put in the work to make it happen.

Before you start visualizing the hot body making a beach debut, you must put in the work, and by "Work" we mean being self-disciplined. The ideas shared in this chapter will not only get you the beach body (or any other thing you want), they will also help you glean a life-long lesson that affects every other area of your life.

Positive thinking plays a very crucial role in helping you develop self-discipline; you will be amazed at the kind of progress you make with this journey when your mind is tailored to think only positive thoughts.

Chapter 5:
Positive Thinking

"Define success on your own terms, achieve it by your own rules, and build a life you're proud to live." -Anne Sweeney

There is a connection between the thought process and discipline, the way a person thinks consistently will affect the kind of progress he/she makes with being self-disciplined. In this chapter, you are going to learn about the crucial role positive thinking plays in helping you become better with discipline.

Every minute you spend thinking about something, you invest in your personality, this investment process works without you knowing it, but over time, you start to manifest the traits of the thoughts you encourage in your mind.

There are two kinds of thought processes; the positive and the negative. Whatever mindset makes you feel good, inspired and encouraged to become a better version of yourself is often birthed through positive thoughts. Of course, the defeatist mentality which makes you think you are undeserving, and incapable is a product of negative thinking.

Anyone presented with both thinking patterns will choose positivity, but it doesn't work that way. You don't get to "Choose" what you want to think about; it isn't something you pick up and use.

Positive thinking is a concept that is adopted and continuously refined through time. Although some people doubt its efficacy, it doesn't undermine the fact that when utilized, you can make a lot of progress with whatever you want to achieve.

You are reading this book because of the keyword "Self-discipline" yet if you can establish a routine that encourages you to think positively, you will get the same results in every other area of your life as well.

Thoughts and Personality

The mind is a force field, it is the most powerful tool humans possess; from within it, thoughts proceed, and these thoughts stir up emotions that affect the quality of life a person lives.

The emotions that come from the mind serve as materials for the formation of words, the words you speak to yourself and others portray your personality. So, if a person exposes his/her mind to negative thoughts, the resulting emotions will be adverse as well which also means that the person's words would be uninspiring even to self.

As this individual try to build self-discipline, there will be trials, because there was no prior training in positive thinking, the person is unable to handle the problems.

At this point, negative words start to pop out "I can't do it" "This habit is going to be the worse of me" "I will struggle with this problem for a long time" "It is just who I am". These are confessions to self that are as a result of negative thoughts, if the effect stopped at just words, one wouldn't be so worried, but it doesn't.

The negative words give way for a very lackluster personality that isn't willing to do anything about a situation. If you struggled with being fit, the negative perception causes you to become lazy.

If you wanted to quit a habit, you would lack the motivation to take the right steps, and the circle continues for anyone who wouldn't kick out negative thinking. The connection between the mind and personality is so strong; you cannot afford to fill your account with the wrong stuff while hoping for the best personality traits. Most striking is the fact that your thoughts become the compass through which you can make progress with discipline.

Strengthen your self-discipline today with positive thoughts, and you will not have to deal with a negative personality. Some people take the right steps towards being self-disciplined; they have a manual of sorts on the subject but cannot reconcile what is written with their life experiences because their personality isn't just right.

The personality issue can be handled by being focused on what you think about the most, what are those thoughts you take to bed with you and the ones you rise within the morning? You've got to be aware of your thinking pattern; it is the only way you can toughen up your personality.

Let the words you say to yourself be a source of encouragement to you on this journey, so this means you've got to fuel your mind with great thoughts that aid the right personality and help you attain self-discipline.

Positive Thinking and Discipline
If you have discussed with a goldsmith, you will discover that the process of creating gold trinkets and pieces of jewelry is a very long one that entails taking the gold substance through fire.

Until gold goes through the fire, it will never be fully formed. Think about self-discipline as gold (what you desire right now) and positive thinking as the fire it must go through to attain perfection.

Self-discipline can be enhanced with positive thinking; you have a responsibility to train yourself by going through the rigorous process of selecting your thoughts.

A person who can fight negative thoughts and win can become a disciplined individual. It takes a lot of self-control to filter your thinking pattern, but you must be committed to this all-important process.

As you strive you think positively, you are also training yourself in the discipline; this is the major idea behind self-discipline and positive thinking. Just like gold, it will take a while for your mind to adjust to a consistent line of thought.

Even when it feels like you have "Arrived" and you are making progress, negative thoughts still try to creep into your mind. The process of kicking out the negative to maintain the positive is likened to building up resistance for self-discipline.

As you fight off negative thoughts, you will also be building up the ability to fight off that bad habit, addiction, problem or challenge that makes it difficult for you to attain self-discipline.

If you always used to think that it was impossible for you to lose weight (this is just an example) before trying to actually "Lose" weight through exercise and dieting, you need to start by replacing the "Can't" with "Can".

Every time the thought of being able to lose weight pops in your head, get rid of it. As you remove the view from your mind, tell yourself that you can do it and start thinking about doing it.

Now, this process will go on for a while, even when you start a diet, negative thoughts remind you that it is possible for you to relapse. The more you get rid of the evil thoughts that weigh you down, the stronger you feel towards achieving your goals, and this is what sets you on course towards being self-disciplined. For some people, they fight off the thought at the initial stages but give in to the temptation of believing the negative ideas.

Gradually such persons begin to doubt their abilities, they don't believe what they can do, and this negative outlook becomes their reality. For people to become stable with their thoughts, they must take proactive measures towards monitoring what they think about.

A person doesn't get to think positive thoughts suddenly, the same way gold doesn't sparkle and shine without going through the fire. There must be a combination of effort and consistency for positive thinking to become a part of a person's mental routine. When a pattern is established in mind, the real battle begins.

Winning the Battle of The Mind

If you succeed with infusing positivity into your thinking process, you have overcome the first challenge with the mind, but there is still so much to do because now, you will be compelled to fight the battle of the mind.

Let's go back to our conversation on gold, shall we? Getting the gold substance itself isn't a guarantee that the goldsmith has got something substantial, yes, it is valuable as gold but what can be made from it? What are the assurances that when made into a piece of jewelry it's going to last long?

So, the gold must go through the fire first. Until the product is tried and tested, there will be doubts and questions. Fire here symbolizes the battle of the mind; everyone who seeks to perfect self-discipline through possible thoughts must win the battle over negative thinking.

Every day presents an opportunity for you to decide and make choices; the process of choosing something over another is where the battle starts to unfold.

If a person has been dealing with pornographic addiction but has been trying to maintain self-discipline through positive thinking, he/she must face the battle of the mind when the temptation to watch porn surfaces.

If the person gives in to the temptation, then it means the battle is lost to negative forces, and self-discipline (which is the prize) cannot be gained at that time. If he/she wins, it translates into a stronger positive mind that can resist porn until the temptation doesn't pop up again.

So what battle are you faced with? Is it the battle of procrastination? Fear of the unknown? Weight loss? Whatever it is, you can win the contest! However, you must have the right tools, and by devices, we are referring to positive thoughts.

Train your mind to reject negative suggestions instantaneously, don't give such thoughts any space or the luxury of time to brood over it.

When you start cutting off little problematic ideas, you will be strengthening and preparing yourself for the larger battle which is often at the decision-making stage.

Some people have remained undisciplined despite reading books and listening to podcasts about how to become self-disciplined not because they were born that way but because they haven't activated the power of their mind.

Now is a great time to start processing positive thoughts, here is a tip you can try out; every night before you sleep; have a rundown of your thought process for the entire day.

If there were negative thoughts, fight them off and replace them immediately with positive thoughts. If you do this daily, you will be repositioning your mind rightly.

Self-discipline can be achieved when a person takes control of his/her mind using a positive thought process. The battle of the mind is real, but you can win with consistent practice, focus and a residue of positive images to replace every negative thought that crosses your mind.

It's All Inside of You!

The most fantastic concept about using thoughts to establish self-discipline is the fact that everything you need to make it happen is within you. You have the most incredible superpower of all time; your mind!

You don't have to rely on anyone else to help you think the right thoughts, come on; it is YOUR mind and your journey towards being self-disciplined. So, you've got to learn how to rely on yourself and bring out so many good thoughts which help you grow from a struggling positive thinker to a stable one.

With some other ideas on how to become self-disciplined, you might require help from someone who will aid your success, but with positive thinking, you are 100% responsible for how it all turns out.

Being fully responsible for your progress means you have more work to do, but it also presents an opportunity for you to remodel your thoughts such that they align with your decision to become a self-disciplined individual. However, you must believe that you've got what it takes; things tend to work better with your plans for discipline when you have faith in yourself.

Regardless of what you are dealing with in your personal life, it is possible to get solutions through positive thoughts. Wake up every morning determined to do better with your thinking process; create images of the successes you enjoy when you start to exhibit self-discipline. These images will serve as alternative materials after you fight off a negative thought.

The Cure to Laziness (This Could Change Your Life)

You want to become better; you want to be the best version of yourself, but you must be self-disciplined first. This means that your involvement is required at every stage. A determined mind doesn't feel inadequate, yes you may struggle at first, but if you hold on to your thought process and belief on how this works for you, there will be progress at the end of the experience.

The entire focus is on you because no one else can "Think" for you, nobody can take your negative thoughts and turn them around. You are also the only one who knows exactly what you think about, and the challenges you are trying to deal with so being the captain of the situation is crucial.

Another reason why you are at the center of this concept is that you are the only one who can be passionate enough to desire changes in your life. It is called "Self-discipline" for a reason, meaning it is all about YOU!

A vital lesson you should get from this chapter is that the power to transform your life lies within you. There are no extra lessons, mentoring sessions or professional help, just you and your thoughts making it through all the negativity and winning.

Be present with your thoughts, never allow yourself to go with a flow of views that are mostly negative. So that means you should be aware of how you think; when it becomes negative, replace it with positive, continue with the process until you achieve a sustainable result with your goals.

If you have always struggled with anything in life, it is because you didn't handle it from within first using your thoughts. Have you ever thought about a person and boom, the person shows up right before you or calls you? It might feel strange at the time, but this is just an example of the power of thoughts.

You can be a self-disciplined person who becomes a source of inspiration to others by fixating your thought process On things that are positive. Positivity yields optimism, even in the face of challenges, you press on knowing that things will get better.

Self-discipline that is obtained through positive thinking is sustainable because it becomes a way of life for you. You get to the point where you no longer struggle with that bad habit; you experience profound changes gradually because everything on the inside of you is correctly aligned with positivity.

You can win the battle against negative thinking, but you must be intentional about it by protecting your mind. Believe in your ability to become a self-disciplined person, trust the process and only accept the best thoughts about yourself.

Identify the events, activities, words and people that trigger negative vibes around, and within you, after identification, you must create a plan that enables you to get rid of the negative indicators (especially the people in that category).

Self-discipline will become a reality when you deal with the challenge of getting rid of negative thoughts. With this process appropriately handled, you can proceed to the next idea which presents a connection between self-discipline and weight loss.

Chapter 6:
The Secret of Self-Discipline and Entrepreneur

"This quality of self-denial in pursuit of a longer-term goal and, indeed, the willpower to maintain the denial, is excellent training for the boardroom." - John Viney

One of the best and highest honors anyone can bestow upon himself is self-discipline. It is the ability of the mind to dictate and control the body, with the heart as a guiding light, leading the way. Self-discipline involves being able to set your heart on something and stick to it religiously, in the face of temptation and distractions. It can be as simple as waking up early, to sticking to only two cups of alcohol per day, to paying a monthly visit to your aged parents.

Self-discipline is not negotiable for an entrepreneur. It should form the basis of your character and guide you to success. You might be lucky to experience short term success when you start a business. This is likely to happen if your product appeals to customers and you are knowledgeable about the business. However, the spice that will keep this success going is self-discipline.

Key Self-Discipline Tactics for Entrepreneurial Success

Many businesses have failed today as a result of a lack of self-discipline, coupled with the right mindset. Maybe failure is an extreme word, but many businesses perform way below their capacity due to an inability of the management to apply due discipline in the needed areas. Many people come up with great ideas, yet they hardly survive and develop effectively to compete.

It is a beautiful thing to be an entrepreneur, however, the word self – discipline is what separates the successful from the unsuccessful. Any business endeavor has many huge and vital components encompassing it. It takes discipline to commit to diligently studying the various areas/segment and committing to it.

In starting a business, many people feel the hardest part is having an idea worth investing in, while the easier part is executing this advice. However, the reverse is the case. There are entrepreneurs out there with terrific ideas. They were brave enough to birth their ideas into business but lack the discipline to grow the business and see it through thick and thin.

This baffles me since building a business is not a herculean task. In this regard, here are some areas of self-discipline that an entrepreneur can apply for business success. The following discusses some discipline you need to apply as an entrepreneur.

Developing A Marketing Plan to Generate A Steady Income Stream

There should be a selling point about your product or services that stands it out from the competition. It is this selling point that you capitalize on when you are trying to advertise which gives you a competitive advantage and a unique selling point.

You should be disciplined enough to offer your customers a benefit that no other ones will. If your business is offering services, for instance, be sure that your services take care of the unique needs of individuals and businesses you will be offering your services to, as no two individual/business are the same. It takes self-discipline to identify this.

Self-Discipline Will Help You to Be Proactive

You can either function through crisis mode or put down modalities to ensure that your business doesn't get dragged into the crisis. What are the proactive measures you have in place to make sure your goal becomes a reality? It is with discipline that you get to adjust early and be able to foresee crisis ahead rather than being reactive to a crisis.

It takes self-discipline with the right mindset to be intentional about your business. Else, you risk crisis and other horrible surprises as well as missing beautiful opportunities.

Self-Discipline to Focus on The Most Important Things Only

You can be so busy with activities yet having nothing tangible to show forth. It takes the right mindset to focus on the right time management practice which will keep you on track and prevent you from getting distracted by low or no value activities. When you define your desired outcome, you will be able to take the necessary steps towards bringing this to reality.

There are project management tools that can help you effectively manage the task, and ultimately manage your time. This keeps your focus on the essentials, keeping you and the team on track. There are also automated processes that can help get rid of distractions.

It Takes Discipline to Think in The Long-Term

Successful businesses are built on relationships. This takes time as the progression will go from 'know' to 'like' and finally 'trust'. A long-term perspective for your business is a sure recipe for success. It, however, takes discipline to let go of instant gratifications in terms of ventures that are not worth investing in.

It Takes Self-Discipline to Take Some Timeout

Establishing a business is a demanding feature that takes time and energy. It is easy to get carried away and neglect family, friends, and even yourself. To be successful, this is non-negotiable. The best part, however, is that entrepreneurship is the only line of job that gives you freedom.

With discipline, you know when to detach yourself from work. Also, self-discipline makes you know when you need to take a step back and catch up with your friends, family and loved ones.

It Takes Discipline to Remain Motivated and Strive for Development

It is vital for entrepreneurs to maintain their motivation. As an entrepreneur, you have got to create and encourage challenges to keep you on your toes and maintain motivation. Also, it takes self-discipline not to relent on your knowledge. Rather, you strive for more knowledge and experience via seminars and refresher courses. With this, you stay current, keep abreast of happenings in your field, which will put you in a good place to drive your business to success.

Self-Discipline Helps Maintain A Team

The importance of teamwork for any business venture cannot be overemphasized. It is vital for any business setting to work in sync. When an entrepreneur encourages teamwork, you can leverage all the talents from your workforce. This will allow you to improve productivity, improve quality and efficiency.

A team activity is like a motor vehicle engine. The various parts of the engines need to work in sync for the vehicle to operate seamlessly.

Daily Self-Discipline Tips for The Entrepreneurs

Anyone can come up with beautiful business ideas. However, staying true and committed to the idea does not come on a platter of gold.

This is what makes successful entrepreneurs stand out. If you take a critical look at successful entrepreneurs, I am pretty sure, they are people that have mastered the art of self-discipline and trained their mindset along the way.

Starting a business is easy, anyone can do that. However, maintaining the business and committing to it such that it stands the test of time is not something that comes naturally. It takes resilience, determination with the right mindset to see a business endeavor to the top.

This doesn't happen in a day, neither does it come in a month. Your success as an entrepreneur is the cumulative effect of all your efforts since inception. In other words, all your inputs affect the success of your enterprise, directly or indirectly.

Since your success as an entrepreneur is a factor of your daily input, it is important to develop the right attitude and mindset essential for success. Here are tips that should be applied daily to bring you nearer to your goal and improve productivity.

1. Don't Get Caught Up with Perfectionism

We understand there is no singular way to execute a project. Hence, when you complete any project, resist the urge to beat yourself up on ways to make it better. When you complete a project, there is a big possibility that a fresh burst of ideas come rushing at you on ways to make or improve the project.

Without self-discipline, you might find yourself starting all over again, leaving you swamped and rushing to meet the deadline. Learn to step back and restrict yourself. It is not as hard as it seems.

2. Keep The 80/20 Rule in Mind

This is known as the Pareto principle or the law of vital few, which states that for many events, about 80% of the effect comes from 20% of the causes. In a business sense, it states that people in a business devote 80% of their time and effort on irrelevancies, and 20% on the important ones.

It takes self-discipline to sit down and realize the truly important task. And even the less important ones can be outsourced or automated. This will allow you to focus on important things which will make your business better off.

3. Dedicate Time to Preparation

It is not all about having your to-do list and schedule for the day. Form the habit of examining it critically and dedicating enough time for each activity. This should not be an excuse to procrastinate, rather, an avenue to reflect and ensure you have all grounds covered.

Be sure to organize your schedule and to-do list in relation to your goal. This little act that sounds rather insignificant can improve your productivity.

4. Detach Your Feelings from The Equation

It takes self-discipline to be able to separate emotions from your enterprise. Many people are so controlled by their emotions and feelings that they wouldn't attempt any task until they feel like it. This is one of the characteristics of procrastination which doesn't have to be so.

There is a big chance that you might never really feel like attempting a task. In this case, what you need is the motivation and zeal to overcome the inertia to get started. Once you begin, you will realize that you just flow along with it. With self-discipline and the right mindset, you can master these emotions and get hold of yourself.

5. Master the Art of Negotiating

As an entrepreneur, this is one of the skills you must really master before you enter the business world. This skill will allow you to get sweet deals on offers and set you up for maximum profit. Besides, it takes discipline to separate emotions from negotiations and business deals. This way, with the right mindset, you will not feel guilty when you negotiate lower prices on your purchases, and you offer high prices when selling. Although, it also takes self-discipline not to offer your services at a price that will be uncomfortable for your customers which might end up backfiring.

6. Develop Mental Toughness

Shall we face it; no one plans for failures, losses, and setbacks in business. However, no matter how proactive and smart you claim to be, these things are sometimes inevitable. This is where resilience, one of the attributes of self-discipline will help you get back on your feet and keep you going.

Your setback could be minimal, and others so huge and it seems like the end of the world. Here is where your stability in the face of a crisis that you have developed through self-discipline coupled with the right mindset will be of great help in helping you survive the storms of the business world.

7. Take Care of Yourself

It is so easy to get caught up in late night meetings. Skipping break-fast is not new to you since you are not so attentive to listen to the rumblings of your stomach. It is easy to work late into the night all in a bid to close the deal and meet the deadline. Many see vacation as a luxury they cannot afford. Yet, all this happens at the expense of your health.

This is where self-discipline comes in. You have got to know when to take a step back and relax. Do away with the stress that comes with running a business. Starting or keeping a business running is very tasking, which makes it so easy to be carried away at the expense of your health. Be sure to take your meals on time, take vacations when due and learn to leave everything work related at work.

In rounding up this chapter, bear in mind that as an entrepreneur, your success depends on a lot of factors/recipes. However, I want you to see self-discipline as the glue that binds all other recipes together. Hence, even with the best employee, a kick-ass idea, unbreakable team spirit, beautiful foresight and first-class training, without discipline, your enterprise is a disaster waiting to happen.

Chapter 7:
The Secret to Self-Discipline and Addiction, Procrastination and Laziness

"Willpower is what separates us from the animals. It's the capacity to restrain our impulses, resist temptation – do what's right and good for us in the long run, not what we want to do right now. It's central, in fact, to civilization." - Dr. Roy Baumeister, Ph.D.

One thing many people with negative vices all acknowledge is the fact that in them lies the power and strength to change their lives for the better. However, due to one thing or the other, they assume and believe that they are not capable of bringing forth that change. This, however, is not so as the major key is to keep working on yourself, overcoming the challenges you meet such that in the future, you look back and are glad of the decision you made.

You don't start and tackle a problem as big as it is. Be specific about your goals and think about the best ways to make it come to reality. A die-hard drunk, for instance, is deceiving himself if he totally cuts himself off from alcohol consumption. He needs to reduce the quantity gradually until he can live safely without being bothered by the cravings. Habits are not formed overnight hence, breaking free of them takes a process – a long, painful and sometimes boring process. This is where the place of self-discipline with the right mindset comes in. Self-discipline will keep you in track when every fiber of your being is crying at you to relapse.

Keep in mind that breaking free from bad habits requires some form of sacrifice. However, I will advise you not to think of it as letting go of something. Addiction to food, nicotine, and porn, etc., pleasures certain parts of the brain. When you are a diehard addict, it is difficult to let go. You will feel you can't get through the day without it.

This is not surprising as humans tend to get comfortable in these vices. They form a comfort zone around these habits hence trying to do away with it doesn't augur well. This is where the power of self-discipline with the right mindset comes in. In breaking free, you need goals and a strategy to achieve your goal. It is self-discipline that will keep you on track when you feel like losing it, and you feel like the walls are crashing down on you.

No matter how difficult it might seem, you can break free. The power lies in you to train your brain and mind to move towards your aim and achieve it. With the power of self-discipline coupled with the right attitude, you can be successful.

With the above in mind, I will discuss powerful strategies to break free from addiction, procrastination, and laziness. We will leverage the power of self-discipline with the right mindset.

Self-Discipline and Breaking Free from Addiction

Breaking free from addiction is more than being determined. Whatever method you choose to break free of your vice, self-discipline is very vital to success. Your goal might be freedom from excess sugar, stopping nicotine use, stopping porn or other substance abuse. While this is possible, long-term success only comes on the wing of self-discipline.

Self-control, one of the important characters you must develop to break free of addiction, also depends on self-discipline. While self-control has more to do about the present, self-discipline allows you to feel the impact of self-control over time.

Self-control will help you make a more rational decision. It will prevent the emotional weight of any situation from influencing your decision making. This explains the ability of people to dissociate stress or other external impulses from inflicting their decision making. This boils back to self-discipline.

Self-discipline is a habit that is learned through determination, dedication, and practice. While it is easy to think that self-discipline will help you through recovery, self-discipline is a habit you must develop and make it stronger and part of you with time.

Self-Discipline and Breaking Free from Addiction

Breaking free from addiction is more than being determined. Whatever method you choose to break free of your vice, self-discipline is very vital to success. Your goal might be freedom from excess sugar, stopping nicotine use, stopping porn or other substance abuse. While this is possible, long-term success only comes on the wing of self-discipline.

Self-control, one of the important characters you must develop to break free of addiction, also depends on self-discipline. While self-control has more to do about the present, self-discipline allows you to feel the impact of self-control over time.

Self-control will help you make a more rational decision. It will prevent the emotional weight of any situation from influencing your decision making. This explains the ability of people to dissociate stress or other external impulses from inflicting their decision making. This boils back to self-discipline.

Self-discipline is a habit that is learned through determination, dedication, and practice. While it is easy to think that self-discipline will help you through recovery, self-discipline is a habit you must develop and make it stronger and part of you with time.

How to Develop Self-Discipline in Recovery?

For people trying to break from the shackles of substance abuse, porn or any vice, self-discipline is not negotiable. It is a vital key to making the journey to self-recovery easy hence guaranteeing a happy and fulfilled life.

Avoid the Triggers

Getting rid of triggers in the form of temptation is crucial to staying sober. The best way is to stay away from triggers. This can come in many forms depending on your type of addiction. Getting rid of all the bottles of alcohols from your fridge, and nicotine, and staying away from some friends for instance, takes determination.

Recovering addicts need the will and discipline to decline outings with old friends. Peer pressure is real and difficult. But making a choice to be rigid and unwavering is critical in the journey to sobriety.

Eat Healthy

Many people struggling with substance abuse often neglect themselves and make horrible food choices. Yet the eating habit has a lot to do about the kind of decision you make. Hence, when in recovery, it is important to commit to healthy meal choices.

This is because there is a link between healthy food and staying sober. With low blood sugar, it is easy to have a foul mood and make poor decisions. Be sure to eat well and see your mealtime as an opportunity to strengthen self-discipline. It will help build resilience that will help with the recovery process.

Embrace The "Wrong"

Over time, excessive dependency on the substance of abuse has reconfigured the brain of the Addict. Hence, he/she sees nothing wrong in a bottle of champagne or cigarette every now and then. Thus, giving in to the demands and cravings of the addiction feels naturally right. However, in the journey to sobriety, there must be a reconfiguration of the brain. This is because the brain thrives based on habits.

As a result of this, you must be willing to work with the "wrong" in your journey to recovery. Since you are incorporating a new set of habits, it might be uncomfortable. This is where self-discipline to stay on track comes in. Humans are wired to hate changes. Hence, your system might rebel against this new-found way of life. With time, practice, consistency and self-discipline, you can retrain your mind to do what is right.

Stay Away from New Addictions

People, in a bid to stay away from addiction, are prone to developing other ones fast. In a bid to fill the void left by sex, porn, or alcohol, they might replace it with excessive eating, nicotine or a variety of other activities.

Herein lies the power of self-discipline. It is with self-discipline and great inner strength that an addict can remain strong and apply moderation to all sectors of their life.

Put Your Thoughts in Order

There is a direct relation between conscious thoughts, stress level and consequent cravings. Most recovering addicts are taught this so that when they get back to the society, they consciously reflect on their self to block every avenue of negative thoughts that could trigger stress which might bring up the addiction.

Stress will arise as you go about your daily activities. There will be people, situations and circumstances to deal with. While you have no power over this, you have every power over your thoughts and with self-control; you can stay positive and keep cravings at bay.

How Self-Discipline Helps with Procrastination

Before we discuss this, it is vital to understand what procrastination is. Procrastination is a habit that arises from a lack of self-control. It arises when our self-control is too low or inadequate to push us to accomplish our goal. We set out to do something, but we do not have the will to overcome the inertia to get the project started.

It is best to see procrastination as a problem, a problem that relates to self-control and self-discipline. It is that lack of self-control that will make it difficult to get the motivation to accomplish what you set out to. Hence, you only find yourself planning to wake up early, to meditate, and to go to the gym. You just cannot seem to get yourself to start out the task. But why do we procrastinate? We lack self-discipline and self-control, it's that simple!

Hence, in fighting procrastination, we need to get to the root of the matter and build up our self-control. A disciplined life is the only tested solution to break the habit. There is no secret formula or magic to help you do away with procrastination.

Since procrastination is a failure in controlling yourself and giving yourself the needed push to overcome work inertia, you need self-control and discipline. It is when you get better at self-control that you will able to get rid of procrastination. Self-control is built with the power and strength of a disciplined life.

How Can You Make Your Life More Disciplined?

Get up early and deactivate the snooze button (if possible), go for a run, make healthy food choices and live a mindful life. When your life is disciplined, your self-control improves, ultimately getting rid of procrastination will be easy. Hence, one of the major keys to beat procrastination is to improve on your willpower. You can develop this by engaging in a minute task every day such as daily meditation, doing the dishes after a meal, making your bed once you get up, and reading a book rather than being on social media. In dealing with procrastination, leveraging on the power of self-discipline, I have these crucial points in understanding and avoiding it.

Identify Excuses and Stop Them

Although not everyone might want to admit it, we all make excuses. Yet, if you do want to get rid of procrastination in your life, you must admit this.

It will have been better if it had stopped at making excuses, but we justify these accuses, allowing the brain to interpret it as normal. We have become so clever and creative that we develop legitimate reasons why we cannot commit to our obligation.

If you will, however, break free from the shackles of procrastination, you must identify and get rid of excuses. Again, it comes back to our sincerity in separating legitimate reasons from mere excuses.

Your Self-Discipline Will Reflect in Your Choices

Someone once said we are a product of our choices. This is one of the attributes peculiar to man. Every blessed day, right from when we open our eyes in the morning, we are faced with choices of whether to wake up or keep sleeping, the type of food to eat, what to wear and whether to meditate or not.

We go about the various task of the day following routines and doing the same thing over and over. Once weekly obligations are done with, we see our free time as a time to our self. This is where the issue lies. The little free time we can get at the end of the day or after each workday, we make sure we dedicate it to relaxation. This is where we leave off other essential things we must do. We put them off and make excuses. Hence, rather than finish the tax report, we will curl up on the sofa and catch up with our favorite football club game.

- This pattern of thinking and lifestyle has got to stop!

To completely rid yourself of procrastination, you need to leverage the power of choice, which still boils down to self-discipline. It is self-discipline that will compel you not to relax and try to reward yourself with "irrelevancies" at the expense of what you really must do.

- You can hit the snooze button, wake up thirty minutes later and rush to work only to fumble at your presentation, or do it right.

- You can fill your intestine with candies, sweet and other sugar-laden substance and deal with obesity and diabetes later or eat healthily and be rewarded with optimum health.

- You can play Xbox all week, crash read and perform woefully at the end of the semester test, or study through the week and get good grades.

- Choices!

Effectively using the power of choices is one way to get rid of procrastination. With self-discipline as your driving force, you can commit to developing your mind, going for a workout, dedicating time to the project etc. You build your self-control and ultimately break free from the grip of procrastination!

Find Your Motivation

No matter how hard you try to do away with excuses, how determined you are to invest your choices wisely, without the right motivation, your effort to do away with procrastination might not stand the test of time.

Hence, a self-disciplined mindset, with the motivation to close a deal will keep a salesman up all night fine-tuning his sales pitch, rather than assuming one way or the other, everything will work out fine.

Bearing the above in mind, you have got to be diligent enough to find your motivation. A student needs the motivation of good grades to keep studying, burning the midnight oil and doing everything necessary to ensure academic success. The motivation of an aspiring Olympic athlete to win a gold medal will keep him on his toes, practicing through thick and thin, when comfortable or not to prepare himself for the event.

When self-discipline is combined with motivation, you are guaranteed to put out the fire of procrastination with ease.

Commence Gradually

Habits are not developed overnight hence; it is foolhardy thinking you can do away with procrastination overnight. You have got to start small and start gradually and take it easy with yourself. Unless your self-control is at its peak, you are bound for failure if you jump at it.

Slowly and steadily, let your life revolve around that healthy habit you want to incorporate. With your motivation and self-discipline, watch as you grow stronger and become rigid in that habit.

Getting free from the shackles of procrastination is a gradual process. With the right weapons in your arsenal, however, you can fast track your way to success and take control of your life. If you find your motivation, self-discipline will keep you going despite all odds.

Self-Discipline and Overcoming Laziness

Humans have this inborn attitude to always seek the easy way out. This expresses itself in the form of laziness when people outrightly shy away from activities. Yet, laziness can become an embargo to your productivity and overall success if appropriate measures are not taken to curb it.

Laziness is an attitude that we all must deal with, especially if we want to go far in life. It is a battle that can serve as a clog in the wheel of progress of anyone. Luckily, the fact that you are on this eBook means you are ready to overcome laziness. Here are some tested tips to overcome laziness:

Think of The Long-Term Effect

When you think about what you stand to gain or lose from doing or not doing a task, it can help make the right decision. The psychological effect of being lazy can serve as an inspiration for getting on your feet and face your task head-on.

This is an effective method because the mind makes better decisions when aware of the long-term effect of any activity. This is an effective strategy that gears people who set goals to do all in their capacity to bring it to realization.

If you can visualize what you stand to gain, how accomplishing your task will make you better off, you have given your mind the needed passion and zeal to get into action. This is a technique that can help clip laziness in its wings for good in your life. That is not all, read on.

Break Your Tasks into Bits

One of the reasons people become lazy is due to the overwhelming nature of the task ahead. Hence, there is this inertia that they can't seem to get rid of. Even with much self-discipline, strenuous activities could be pretty discouraging. This discouragement produces a sort of psychological effect on the brain, where the natural balance is disturbed.

In a bid to restore sanity, the brain would suggest that you put off the task. This is where laziness sets in. The best way to constructively counter this is to divide the tasks into bits. Let yourself know that you will not tackle it at a stretch.

For instance, I read a book on intermittent fasting some time back. The book talked about not eating for about eight hours at a stretch. Everything in me cried against this. However, when I got to the portion that recommended taking water and other forms of juice, I was relieved. Also, the portion that advised I can start with a 5 hour fast and gradually extend the hours was a big encouragement.

In the same way, confronting your task this way reduces the tendency of being overwhelmed which could help curb laziness.

Reduce Distractions

There are so many distractions (for instance social media) vying for our attention that committing on a task is usually hard. While advancement in tech has been a blessing, it has its fair share in contributing to people's laziness.

This is because there is pressure to keep up with social media, update status or impress people with social media pictures and posts. This is where discipline comes in. Centuries ago for instance when there were minimal distractions, productivity was high, reducing the tendency to have divided attention.

To deal with laziness, one of the most effective tips is to cut off other unproductive activities that compete for your time. This explains why specialists would advise you to stay away from the TV for the rest of your life and kill your social media activities. While this might be extreme, the best approach is to minimize distractions.

How Do You Reduce Distractions?

Have a leisure time: The distraction to keep up with social media contributes to laziness and affects productivity. While deactivating social media accounts sounds extreme, we recommend you have a scheduled time. This is where the self-discipline to resist the urge to check FB notification comes in.

Have a Not-to-do list: You're not-to-do list a list of all activities that are an embargo to the fulfillment of your task. For instance, it is not practical to write that you will visit your old parents today. Rather, make a list of all activities that could prevent you from visiting your parents. Hence, you can say: I will not take a nap today or, I will not spend more than two hours on my PC.

The idea behind a not-to-do list is to see clearly the things that compete for your time. These are likely to prevent you from committing to the task at hand. Identifying this helps put you on the path of success to curb laziness.

Avoid Being Too Hard on Yourself

You admit you could be lazy, and you are on a quest to get help, terrific!

You have seen how laziness has cost you and you are out to overcome it. However, you get disappointed at times when you fall short. This might be pretty discouraging when it happens, and you try to beat yourself up for falling short of expectation.

In contrast to being hard on yourself and beating yourself up, I advise that you attempt something else. Praise yourself; give yourself kudos for the efforts. The brain is likely to respond effectively and be motivated to positive reinforcement rather than scolding yourself. Whenever you fall short of expectations, be sure to attempt this.

Cultivate Self-Discipline

In trying to overcome laziness, I will use this illustration to show the impact of self-discipline. Consider all the efforts and tips listed above as all the parts of a motor vehicle engine. Look at self-discipline as the engine oil that keeps every other part running smoothly and in order. Without engine oil, a vehicle engine is headed for destruction.

In other words, the tendency of all the tips discussed above to produce a result is very low if not accompanied by self-discipline. It is self-discipline that can help you think in the long-term. It is self-discipline that will allow you to put off distractions, schedule a time for social media, and abide by it religiously. It is only self-discipline that can help you leave instant gratification and think of the long-term effect and consequences of your actions and choices.

You can overcome laziness. It will, however, happen on the wings of self-discipline, coupled with the right mindset.

Chapter 8:
The Secret to Self-Discipline and Weight Loss

"Willpower is the key to success. Successful people strive no matter what they feel by applying their will to overcome apathy, doubt or fear." - Dan Millman

The desire to lose weight tops the list of what most people want which inspires them to become self-disciplined. Aside from the thrill of having a sexy body, there are a lot of health benefits to be gained from losing weight, but it wouldn't happen without consistent effort.

People who struggle endlessly with weight loss do not have an organized plan of action; they want to lose weight, they want to do whatever it takes to achieve their goal, but because of the absence of organization, their wishes are not attained.

It takes a lot of self-discipline for a person to start the process of weight loss and continue in it even after they get to their desired weight because fitness should be a significant aspect of everyone's life. You shouldn't consider weight loss only when you want to shed some pounds, make it a permanent part of your life.

The Cure to Laziness (This Could Change Your Life)

In a previous chapter, there was a section on habits and how those routine activities you do affect the quality of your life. From that chapter, you gained insight into how you can create better practices and the same message resonates in this section as well.

Until you intentionally incorporate the right habits into your life, your weight loss idea will be nothing but a dream.

While the central focus of this chapter isn't on patterns, you should have the concept in mind as you read because, in the end, you must adjust with your habits for sustained weight loss experience.

Habits are a part of you, but plans are ideas you should implement that will help you achieve your goals. For you to be self-disciplined, you need a combination of habits and methods. So, what can you do?

Firstly, you should get an organized plan that will help you keep track of your purpose and then make these plans a part of your habit by doing them repeatedly.

Being able to lose weight through regular exercise is a plan, using the staircase at the office instead of the elevator can become a habit inspired by the initial idea to exercise regularly.

When there is an agreement between your plans and habits, self-discipline becomes possible. You wouldn't struggle to go to the gym, eat healthy, stay off calories or eat in portions. All of these can be adequately managed using the principles of time maximization.

Manage Your Time

Even when you start to make plans a part of your habit, if you are not conscious of how to use time, you will still have issues. One of the secrets to being self-disciplined and lose weight is to use time wisely; you will not get an extra minute, second or hour.

Everyone has the same amount of time yet why do some people make progress more than others?

The reason you feel lazy and too tired to head to the gym in the morning is probably because you didn't use your time well the previous day which is why you went to bed late. So, every time you don't use your time wisely, there is a ripple effect of your inaction snowballing into the rest of the day.

Taking charge of your time isn't just to lose weight, yes this is what you want to achieve now, but there is so much more than you can do with proper time management. As you lose weight, you will also observe that there are other significant changes taking place in your life simultaneously.

But back to weight loss, you can achieve your goal with effective time management; Don't do the things that aid weight loss when it is convenient for you, your goal should propel you to schedule your time, making room for important activities that bring you closer to your dream.

A daily planner will be handy at this point, sit down the day before a new day and plan. Set time aside for the regular things you do (your job, family time) and then create a separate schedule for the weight loss activities you want to do for that day.

For example, plan to wake up in the morning and go for a run, drink water, take a healthy breakfast, get to work and use the stairs. At lunchtime, enjoy veggies and get back home in the evening for some yoga. Have an early dinner and turn in early for sleep as well.

With a plan, you know exactly what to do every time, and you are motivated to doing it because the activities are interwoven with every other action lined up for your day.

Your ability to schedule your time and stick to the plan is a testament of your growth with being self-disciplined. Set a specific target for yourself; when do you want to lose weight? How many pounds do you want to drop? What can you do weekly that brings you closer to the milestone?

You will carry out weight loss tasks with a sense of urgency when you have precise objectives to attain. It is your responsibility to achieve the goals you set on this journey to fitness and health. How does a person become responsible for their life?

Take 100 Percent Responsibility for Your Life

Did you know that it is possible to have the answers to weight loss and not make as much progress as you desire? Oh, it is possible, and it isn't because of anything you did wrong, sometimes it's just a function of your body.

Some people will complain, scream and murmur about their inability to shed weight at a breakneck pace. As they complain, they try to lay the blame on someone or something else, their nutritionist, the food, gym instructor, their boss, etc.

Complaining and blaming others isn't a sign of being responsible, it just shows how undisciplined you are. You've got to take 100% responsibility for your life today!

Things will go well with you sometimes, and then they may not go well with you some other times, in good or bad seasons, you are responsible for your life. Do not resort to complaints that do not change anything, don't blame the world of its system for issues you can resolve.

One of the hallmarks of self-disciplined individuals is their ability to stay calm when their dreams don't happen the way they want it to. Such persons realize that if something isn't working, they can improve on it instead of grumble about it.

The Cure to Laziness (This Could Change Your Life)

You are the custodian of your dream and society will not be held responsible should that dream wither away. Get yourself together, be bold to face challenges with a solution-oriented mind. It is easier to complain about something that isn't working than to act on it, but the pathway to greatness is never secure.

Responsibility births self-discipline; start to do the things required of you without anyone forcing you to do them and regardless of the outcome, keeping working at it.

Being responsible also helps you identify your areas of weakness, maybe you've not been going to the gym because you don't like the treadmill.

Well, when you take responsibility for your results (when they are negative), it causes you to reflect on what went wrong. Upon discovering that you don't like the treadmill, you can change it and stick to what you want.

Don't complain when faced with challenges, discipline your mind to provide solutions if problems spring up. Placing the blame on someone else or an institution is irresponsible.

Responsibility also comes with awareness; you become conscious of the fact that everything you have achieved can be replicated into the future. This means you need to consider long-term plans.

Think Long-Term

The people you admire who exhibit self-discipline weren't born that way, and they certainly didn't attain the level of discipline they show by sticking to routines occasionally.

Convenience and pleasure are two ideas that will affect your journey to being self-disciplined if you don't handle them early enough. Long-term dreams are not done conveniently; they are also not done when there is time or when you "Can", you do them because you NEED to.

More so, doing things out of pleasure will not help you lose weight, neither will it make you a self-disciplined person. People who focus on what gives them pleasure forfeit their progress for a short-term feeling.

The fact that you love pizza and the spicy sensation it gives doesn't mean you should take it every day especially if you want to lose weight. The feeling pizza gives you is short-term, it probably wouldn't exceed 24 hours - is this short experience worth the entire dream to lose weight?

You have an opportunity to build something sustainable from today by acting in alignment with your long-term goals. It doesn't matter if you love potato chips so much, so long as it isn't healthy for you, don't indulge it. Always think about how you want to be in the future, create an image in your mind and hold on it.

The next time you are tempted to decide based on short-term gratification, remember the image you created and do something concrete that counters the short-lived feeling.

The concept of self-discipline is also a lasting idea because whatever you want to get rid of needs to stay out for a long time. From pornographic addiction to weight loss, procrastination, etc. - once you overcome these issues, you wouldn't want to go back to the experience again.

Set goals that go beyond what you can enjoy today; remember that long-term achievements are always inspiring even to yourself. You will look back years later and be grateful for the sacrifices you made in the past.

Self-discipline is refined over time and strengthened to resist even bigger temptation but if you start now, if you begin the process of building long term experience, you will become a disciplined person.

Weight loss will be just one of your several achievements because self-discipline for long-term dreams helps you accomplish other things as well. The reason some people might not sustain the long-term approach because they do what is "Easy" instead of doing what is "Right".

Do What's Right, Not What's Easy

There is a thin line between what is right and what is easy such that some people don't know the difference between both concepts. If you pay close attention to your weight loss journey, you will get to know what is right and what is easy making it easier for you to make the right decisions.

Here's a scenario that explains the concept of right and easy: eating just about any food is natural, you can pick up anything from anywhere and eat, this is easy.

What is right on the other hand is to deliberately watch what you eat because eating anything from anywhere is indeed not healthy for your body.

The easy things are always fun, they make you feel free, but you are giving up your freedom without knowing it. Many people do what is easy, they are comfortable with it and wouldn't want to consider anything else.

So, if everyone around you is doing what is easy instead of what is right, change the course of your activities. The most natural things don't take a lot of mental exercises; they are like reflexes, you do them and guess what, they give you zero results. You should do things that align with your goals, in fact, this is how you know what you're doing is right; it takes you closer to your goal.

Your dreams will become a reality when you always do the right things, not the easy ones. The right stuff strengthens your resolve to win; they help you appreciate the weight loss process.

You can "Plan" to do the right things; you can create a schedule that makes you stick to the right events especially when the temptation to slip into easy activities abounds around you.

Learn to stick to the proper routines, create an atmosphere of possibilities around you that limits your choices to only the right ones. If it is so easy for you to avoid the gym so, bring the gym to your home; purchase the equipment and set them in your bedroom. As you wake up in the morning, you don't get to take the easy route; you start the right activity by taking on the gym equipment.

What are those natural things you do that contradict the positive efforts you make? What kind of activities comes naturally to you but aren't healthy? Identify those easy problems and be disciplined enough to kick them out.

Have A PLAN

Creating a plan works with everything! If you are going to get positive results with anything, first create a plan. Especially now that you are on the journey to weight loss, you've got to plan how to eat, what to eat or drink, how to exercise and the things to avoid.

Self-discipline can also be attained when you have a plan; if you stick to what you create, you will get the desired result. Now with this concept, you have got to be very practical and hands-on with the process.

There are a lot of mobile apps that are designed to help people plan for weight loss and some of these apps also make it possible for you to be accountable every day.

If you want to use a manual diary, you must first create the plan (daily or weekly) and create a column for "Daily comments" where you fill out what you did in comparison with what you were supposed to do.

So, at the end of every day, you were using your planner, you can ascertain the areas where you perform excellently as well as the aspects you can work on.

It takes a lot of discipline to stick to a plan, yes, a lot of people know the importance of planning but how many make it work? So, you will be winning on all fronts with this tip; you get to lose weight, become self-disciplined and create a better pattern that adds value to your life.

Planning also makes you do things deliberately so if you want to be intentional about what you do, if you're going to be self-disciplined without feeling so pressured, if you're going to lose some pounds, you need to start to making PLANS towards these goals today.

The Cure to Laziness (This Could Change Your Life)

The desire to lose weight can be more than a wish, and it can come to fruition when you put in the work and do what is required of you. This chapter has shown you how possible it is to set weight loss goals and attain them using the right principles.

For you to achieve anything in life, you must attain some level of discipline and then gradually build on it until you become consistent with it. With weight loss, you can start by being disciplined enough to eat in portions, but you shouldn't remain at this level for too long.

Progressively work towards going beyond just eating in portions by getting off an unhealthy diet entirely instead of just taking them in servings. You may start by taking a walk around your house, improve on that by running, jogging and even getting a gym membership.

As you gradually build on self-discipline, you will be able to stretch your habits, create new plans and stick to purposeful living. If you try to do it all at once, you will not get as many results as you would when you follow a process.

Some of the notions shared in this book are still plans, they are concepts with the excellent potential to work for you if you make them a part-habit. Be committed to the programs and they will become habits, enjoy the patterns and they will lead you to your dreams.

As you implement the suggestions, remember that weight loss isn't the goal; being fit and healthy is the objective. After shedding some pounds, some fall back to the same unhealthy routines and eating life-style, making the entire process unfruitful.

If you are going to enjoy the best of being self-disciplined, you must consider the long-term plan. There are sustainable, long-lasting disciplined habits you can incorporate daily that will make a difference with you on this journey. Flip over to continue your lessons.

Chapter 9:
Long-Term Self-Disciplined Habits

"One Painful Duty Fulfilled Makes the Next Plainer and Easier." -
Helen Keller

Self-discipline is a long-term project that entails consistently building up certain habits which make it easier for you to take charge of your life. From the information you've gathered in previous chapters, you understand the crucial role that habits play in helping individuals become self-disciplined.

However, habits must become like a second skin to individuals for sustainable results. It isn't enough to imbibe the habits "Until" you become a disciplined person, you've got to incorporate the practices into every area of life by infusing them into your daily routine.

If the concept of habits for self-discipline is fully integrated, you are bound to make a lot of progress with your life goals.

You don't have to read more about how essential habits are so, just read on as you discover the most results-driven habits that can change your narrative for long-term impact.

You will observe that some of the habits shared in this chapter are straightforward ideas and concepts anyone can implement, which means that attaining self-discipline isn't a complicated process.

More so, the impact habits have on your life isn't determined by the simplicity or complexity of the pattern. By doing what is required of you, permanent changes can start to take place in your life.

Developing a goal-setting habit gives you something worth fighting for such that even in the face of challenges, you are steadfast towards achieving your set goals.

Define A Goal Worth Fighting For

Creating habits without having a definite purpose in mind will cause you to be unstable. First, define a goal you want to achieve, it must be a goal that adds value to your experience when it is completed.

Think about something you've always wanted to do and then set it in your heart as a goal. Next, the goal needs to be deconstructed; this entails breaking down all the pieces of the purpose so you can deal with one piece at a time. If your goals are to lose weight, for example, you've got to break down the essential parts of the goal into the steps you will need to take to accomplish your desired pressure.

As you deconstruct the goal, remember to attach an action plan for each piece, something you can do every day that brings you closer to the goal. Now your responsibility is to ensure that you stick to these action plans one day at a time.

Try not to skip any activity or meal plan that will help you achieve your goal and be committed to doing this for the long haul. This is an example of a lasting habit that encourages self-discipline in a person.

Prioritize the Goal

Before anything else, make sure your goals are prioritized; whatever you do every day should be inspired by the visualization of your objectives. When something becomes top priority, you make it work regardless of the challenges you are faced with.

Rank your goals in order of importance; whatever is most important to you should get all the attention at first. On the other hand, depending on what the actual goal is, you can start with smaller goals; as you succeed with these smaller ones, you will be motivated to take on the bigger goals.

When working with goals, timing is everything. Organize your goals around specific times, so you have deadlines to work with. Do you want to lose weight? How many pounds should go in six months?

After dealing with the smaller goals, you can focus on the top priorities. Devote time from your daily routines to do make the dream a reality; every little step you take matters.

When you start to focus on your prioritized goals and follow your plan religiously, you will be building a habit of consistency that helps you become a disciplined person.

Find Role Models Who Inspire You

Sometimes achieving a goal can be more comfortable when you have role models that encourage you daily. There are people who have walked a similar path like you now and those who have experienced the same trials and won.

You must seek out such individuals because they are the role models that will inspire you to strive for success even in the face of daunting challenges continually. Whenever you want to be so hard on yourself, remember that these role models stumbled some time, but they picked themselves up and moved on.

People who have survived the worse of what you are going through right now are all around you, reach out to them, make a connection and learn from their stories. Some of them might not be in your country, and maybe online via social media.

What are you waiting for? Join them on social media, subscribe to their newsletters, listen to their podcasts, watch their YouTube videos, etc. As you listen, read or watch their content, you will find answers to some Of the issues you deal with and use the answers to strengthen your new habits. While applying the solutions they proffer, you will be building up self-confidence as well.

If the role models you seek are within your immediate environment, you should reach out. Politely ask for a meeting and share your experience while taking note of the suggestions, life lessons and ideas the role model shares with you.

Failure: Even for A Day, Is an Option

The fact that you are creating long-term habits for a self-disciplined life doesn't mean you are immune to failure. Yes, you want to win at all cost, and you are determined to make it work but come on, humans are bound to make mistakes and fail.

It isn't the failure that counts; it's how you respond to it and what you make of it that matters. If you create a plan to perfect a habit for a month and you don't keep up with the idea for a day, it is okay.

Wake Up the Following Day and Make It Work!

Failure is also a learning process; you've got to embrace it and own up to it. Your milestones may not come full circle all the time, but it doesn't mean you aren't making progress. Be open to anything that happens during the process even if it is a mistake.

Keep Track of Your Progress

Failure or not, you are making progress, and you must keep track of it. Having a plan is different from sticking to it; so, by keeping track of your progress, you will be making sure that you follow up with your project.

Get to know how far you've come with your new habits, the areas you need to work on and how you can add some value to the process going forward. If you are not keeping tabs on your progress, you will be unstable with the plans you set up.

When you went to school, you had to write a lot of tests and examinations because the teacher wanted to know if you understood all you've been taught. Without those tests and exams, you wouldn't have made it to the next level of your education.

So, do you see why progress reports are critical? They help you monitor all you do and keep you in check. Keeping track of your progress also creates an opportunity for improvement in areas you haven't performed well.

As you keep track, you also discover the differences between what you are doing right now and what you are "Supposed" to do. The former is always convenient but may not be the right thing while the latter is what gets you the desired results.

Set Monthly Milestones

Setting a monthly benchmark is a habit everyone should incorporate. Having goals is a good thing but having landmarks that help you stick to your goals is even better.

If you want a long-term goal that may take up to six months, you will need monthly milestones that keep you focused throughout the period you try to attain the goal. Split the goal into monthly achievements, work towards making sure the monthly sub-goals are met and assess your progress at the month's end. Sometimes your goals may be too big for you, in fact, you might feel overwhelmed by them, and this is normal.

But by cultivating the habit of breaking down goals into monthly milestones, you will be able to handle your aspirations in the most confident and timely manner yet. Using milestones also help you become a disciplined person who is conscious of the fact that there must be a monthly progress report at the end of the month.

So, you strive to do the needful every month until the completion of the goal. Milestones also keep you focused, fully engaged and committed to your goals.

Self-Analyze Your Progress

As you take steps toward your goals every day, you need to pause at some point to analyze your progress. Getting to know how far you have come will help you determine what you can do to become even better.

Some people become consumed with the idea of making progress that they don't even know when they aren't attuned to the plan anymore. It is okay to take a break and observe some moments of self-introspection, these moments help you appreciate the progress you've made and serves as an opportunity for you to make plans concerning the areas that aren't perfect.

Monitoring your progress is an avenue for you to observe the patterns that work for you and the ones that don't. If you have been doing things the wrong way, you will discover why and then you can also strengthen the effort you put into making your goals become a reality.

If you made time to plan, then you will have the material that will serve as a reference point for you to analyze your progress. Check your plans; match the ones you wrote to the ones you achieved and find out why others weren't realized.

At the end of your self-analysis, you will experience increased motivation to take on better habits and do more towards achieving your goals.

Remove Negative Habits

While analyzing your progress, take the time to obliterate negative habits. You are trying to instill the right habits that will help you become a disciplined person, but you will not achieve the proper habits when you still got the negative ones hovering all around you.

At this stage, everything you do should be in sync with the new habits you are trying to formulate. You know the habits you struggle with; you know the activities that cause you to take steps backward in your quest to be disciplined.

Well, go beyond identifying bad habits and start getting rid of them. The old habits will not make your transition process easier nor will they help you achieve your goals. Those negative habits you are struggling with can make an early exit at this stage because you are implementing a lot of changes with your habits now. However, don't expect the bad habits to disappear; you've got to work towards it making this a reality.

For every bad habit you want to remove, prepare to replace it with a good practice that becomes a part of your new goal plan. Show how disciplined you can be by kicking out unproductive habits and retaining the good habits that inspire you to become better.

Keep Pushing For 30 Days Straight

If you can keep up with a pattern for as long as 30 days, you can be sure that you have gained the mastery over it. The habits and ideas shared in this chapter will only become impactful when you are committed to doing them regularly.

Having the 30-day goal in mind helps you maintain focus; you wake up daily knowing that you've got fewer days left and time is running out. When you create your "Goal plan" make sure it cuts across 30 days.

Within the plan, have sections that contain action plans for the first five, fifteen and twenty-five days. By the time you get to the twenty-ninth day, you should be able to have a progress report.

Following a 30-day plan is a recipe for long-term discipline you will be building yourself to achieve your goals at the same time. When creating your unique 30-day plan, the first seven days should be about simpler tasks that help you ease into the habit. After these first seven days, take things up a notch by the second week and continue to raise the bar until the last day.

By the thirtieth day, if you were strict with adhering to the plan, you will have amazing results to show for the hard work, dedication and commitment. Life can be very easy, fun-filled and inspiring if you create a system that works. Through your habits, it is possible to live your best life today as you fight off negative experiences that are enhanced by being undisciplined.

For some people, they enjoy the benefits of having the right habits for only a short period and in that amount of time, they attest to the impact it has over their lives. The reason such person relapses and become undisciplined again is that they didn't build up sustainable, long-term habits.

The information shared with you in this section repositions you for success in life. The addictions and problems you struggled with in the past will no longer hold you down because you've consolidated your habits with your daily routines.

The initial challenge with building long-term habits is keeping up with the pattern every day, therefore the 30-day milestone must be taken seriously. If you can sustain the same process for 30 days, then you've got it for life! Work towards achieving the 30-day plan and watch your habits become increasingly progressive such that being disciplined isn't a struggle anymore.

Chapter 10:
The 3 Proven Methods

*"I used to walk down the street like I was a superstar... I want peo-
ple to walk around delusional about how great they can be – and
then to fight so hard for it every day that the lie becomes the truth."*
- Lady Gaga

Some ideas are so simple to handle when thinking about self-disci-
pline, you need to apply them to your peculiar experience and watch
them work. However, most of these "Simple" steps aren't always ad-
equately harnessed, they can be overlooked for the more complex
ones, and this must change.

This chapter introduces you to three powerful yet straightforward
methods that will transform your life in the most amazing ways pos-
sible. They are the three proven techniques that will shape you into
the man or woman you want to be.

But the idea behind having "Tips" and "Steps" shouldn't deter you
from creating more out of the box ideas that work for you. For

instance, you may want to utilize these techniques for a specific challenge, but that doesn't mean you can't use them for something else.

Every idea, suggestion, concept, or plan you have read through in this book can change your life's narrative completely in more ways than one.

So, while keeping your eyes on the specific goal you've got for your life, remember that you can cause a change with other areas of your life, but first do you know who are?

Know Your Identity

It is easy to assume; you know who you are, after all, you have been living your life for so many years now right? Well, this assumption is always erroneous because there are still a lot of people who do not have a firm grasp of their identity.

Knowing who you are is crucial to achieving your long-term goals. When you are self-aware, you tend to do things that are in sync with your dreams. Your journey to being self-disciplined will be a successful one based on how well you know yourself.

You wouldn't want to quit habits because other people are doing it, neither will you want to establish new patterns for others. Everything you do will be inspired by your desire to fill the gaps in your life because you know who you are now.

When you know who you are, it also becomes increasingly comfortable for you to shift your thoughts such that you don't go back to the wrong things.

If you are dealing with laziness and a desire to be fit, a discovery of who you are will propel you to take strategic steps towards curtailing laziness.

More so, you will think and believe that you are not a lazy person because that is what self-discovery does. Your words and actions will be tailored towards fighting off laziness because unlike in the past, you are empowered with information and greater knowledge about yourself.

How Can You Start on The Path to Self-Discovery?

Firstly, what are your values? What are those things you hold dear to you? The ideas you know you will never compromise your values, and values are motivating factors that keep you going even when you are down and out. Take some time to discover your values and align them with your long-term goals.

Another way to know your identity is through your interests; these are your passions, hobbies or anything that draws your attention. The things you are curious and concerned about constitute your interests. This idea is so important because when you know the things that interest you, they take you closer to your goals.

The Cure to Laziness (This Could Change Your Life)

Of course, your temperament also matters when knowing your identity. Some people struggle with being self-disciplined because they don't know their character. You've got to see if you are a people's person, an introvert, extrovert, an organizer, etc.

Think about this for a moment; a person is trying to lose weight, he/she has been going to the gym and other fitness places with many people but hasn't made any real progress. After each session at the gym, the person feels like it was all a waste of time and cannot wait to get out of the crowd.

Over time, this person stops going to the gym and forgets about the weight loss goal. Well, the problem here is that the person hasn't discovered his/her identity through the temperament.

It is possible that this individual is an introvert and tends to learn faster alone. By continually going to the gym where there are a lot of people, the individual will not achieve his/her goals.

On the brighter side, if this person takes the time to discover his/her identity, to know who he is and embraces it, fitness sessions can take place at home with sustainable and long-term results.

You can discover your identity by getting to know your strengths and weaknesses, we all have areas of greatness and some flaws. Identifying the fields, you are extremely good at will help you achieve a whole lot within a short time as opposed to doing things you aren't so good at and not making anything.

Be honest with your assessment of self in discovering your strengths and weaknesses; this idea will be constructive when you try to take steps towards achieving your goals. However, life is continually evolving, and you change periodically, the areas of weakness can become stronger points for you and vice versa. The key to knowing your identity and utilizing the information for self-discipline is so you can stay true to yourself.

Don't be something you are not, embrace every aspect of your life as you strive to become better daily. Spend time with yourself, ask questions, observe your decision-making process and you will get to know your identity. But it doesn't end with knowing who you are; there are other concepts you must also consider for long-term results as a disciplined individual.

Use Reward and Punishment

Now that you know who you are, you will be more inclined to start doing the right things that inspire you on this journey to self-discipline. But there is a challenge with doing the right thing; some people do not take the right steps seriously despite the knowledge that these steps will add value to them.

So, it is possible for a person to know that drinking a lot of water is healthy and not try to drink because he/she doesn't want to. This attitude breeds incompetence and laziness; it also makes it difficult for anyone to make progress with an idea.

It is not cool for you to self-sabotage your journey. You know why you want to be a disciplined person so why aren't you doing what is required? Why do you deliberately ignore the process because there are no consequences?

Until you start to utilize the concept of punishment and rewards, you may struggle for a long time with your aspirations despite knowing what to do.

Everything you have read from the introductory section until now has prepared you for a self-disciplined life, so you have the tools and ideas you should implement. If you set up a daily, weekly or monthly plan, be mindful of how you execute your programs.

If you carry out your plans for a period, then reward yourself for a job well done. Your reward can be something that also reinforces the bigger idea you are trying to accomplish or something that motivates you to become better.

You shouldn't wait until you accomplish something grand before rewarding yourself. If you start with a milestone, upon completion reward yourself, it might be a high-five, some words of kindness to yourself or a tap on your back.

When you attain a more significant milestone, do something you've always wanted to do for yourself, something that motivates you such that you can do much more about achieving your goals. Rewards are excellent concepts that give you a significant boost, they make you believe in yourself, and this is a major propelling factor for anyone who wants to achieve success in life.

There is a flip side to gaining rewards, and it is punishment. Just as you are quick to reward yourself when you do the right things, be swift with punishment when you don't. You don't need an accountability partner to tell you when you should be punished, what you need is to be stern with yourself.

How important is the goal you want to achieve? If it is essential, then you should be prepared to punish yourself for not sticking to the processes that will make you attain the goal. Instead of giving yourself something you always dreamed about as you did with benefits, you should withdraw some privileges.

Sometimes, you may have to resort to high negative punishments that cause you to realize how far you have derailed from the goal. The activities you enjoy should be cut short so you can focus on the bigger picture.

The times of punishment will also serve as a reminder that your commitment to excellence cannot be compromised. After several punishments and deprivations, you will be strategically positioning yourself for more productive ventures that will bring you closer to your dreams.

You should strike a balance between reward and punishment, if you are going to be extreme with one, do the same for the other. Being overtly radical with discipline and not doing the same for rewards can lead to discouragement.

For you to avoid being discouraged, you might want to maintain a balanced approach to both ideals such that there is room for second chances and opportunities to try again till you perfect the process.

If you continue with this pattern, you will arrive at a level where you don't have to punish yourself to get things done. You do the right things every day because you have programmed your mind to stick to the steps that guarantee success. At the end of the day, because of the reward/punishment process, you will be empowering yourself to shatter glass ceilings and become an inspiration to others.

Set Yourself Up for Success

One of the products of the reward/punishment system is that it sets you up for success. By following through with the things, you need to do to avoid punishment and gain rewards; you will be motivated to them without such consequences.

By setting yourself up for success, you will be able to take steps towards your dreams without being prompted to; it all just happens naturally. This level of success doesn't occur spontaneously, it takes time to build and maintain, but it is always worth it in the end.

Success is an idea; it is never finite. You must continually press forward to make it happen, but the process to embracing that idea requires a lot of work, and this entails you doing what should be done regardless of your moods, feelings or affiliations at the time.

You must plan your future today by telling those stiff challenges to crumble before you by taking decisive actions towards your goals. You have the first steps already by learning about yourself and knowing what you want out of life, but it doesn't stop at knowing.

Devote your time and energy to those goals that are meaningful, we are talking about strategy here. Setting up for success means you are aware of what you want and then you are creating a strategy towards accomplishing it.

Decide to move onwards and say, "I don't want to know how hard this is, I am not letting go until I get the best out of this situation". By saying the most inspiring words to yourself, more effort is required, and it can be achieved by utilizing one word: FOCUS!

At this stage, you transcend the feeling of seeking rewards or averting punishment; you are convinced of the potency of the process that you find yourself doing them daily by being focused.

The Cure to Laziness (This Could Change Your Life)

Focus means setting your sights on the results even before kickstarting the process; it means doing what is required and moving beyond mistakes or future worries. Focus helps you become an exceptional person who isn't seeking perfection but making continuous effort towards one goal. You will be confident in your strengths and self-worth knowing that you can fix any problem.

You must learn how to set yourself up for success by taking charge of your life and make the necessary changes when required. Create realistic strategies and stick to them even in difficult times.

Dreams will never become real until you intentionally set yourself for success. If you converse with someone who has achieved remarkable things, you will observe that they did two things effectively; they set goals and created a pathway that connects them to the targets.

Now, these successful people stick to that pathway regardless of what happens, they have big dreams and do not set limits. Don't listen to great people and forget to implement what you learn; their stories should serve as a springboard for your dreams.

Tell yourself that if they did it, you could do it also. Remember to become passionate about what you believe in; sometimes passion is what keeps you focused; passion will always help you get to your destination.

The process of setting yourself up for success requires a lot of discipline, but when you succeed with it and start implementation, you will become self-disciplined and self-motivated.

While anticipating the results of your goals, live in the reality of it happening; you will be setting yourself up for success when you do. In addition to all you've learned in this book, make good use of these three proven methods. When you know who you are, it becomes easy to set yourself up for success while taking measures to discipline yourself when you fall short of expectations.

Think about the area of life where you need more motivation; how can these methods help you improve? When you take the lessons gained and make them a part of your life, it becomes easy for you to experience changes and positive results.

After you get the results you desire from the challenges you want to change, continue to apply these techniques for a more robust experience. Self-discipline isn't attained when you no longer suffer from the addiction or the issues you battle with.

You don't get the assurance of discipline because you have lost weight; you achieve it by surpassing your goals. Self-discipline is a product of continuous efforts, application of techniques and steps taken to uplift oneself daily. The idea that one step makes you attain discipline is often misleading, so use these three methods provided in this section to change the narrative of your experience.

The Cure to Laziness (This Could Change Your Life)

Changing the narrative also means taking control of your life and living on your terms. It means acknowledging the fact that there may be issues to deal with, but you are ready to stick to your beliefs and succeed. More information about how you can take charge of your life is in the next section.

Chapter 11:
Taking Control of your Life

"The ability to subordinate an impulse to a value is the essence of the proactive person." - Stephen Covey

A person doesn't become self-disciplined without being in control. The concept of gaining control over one's life must be embraced and practiced by everyone because it is a necessary factor for success with discipline. Everything you have read in this book was intentionally put together to help YOU. It doesn't matter if you share this experience with someone else, that person cannot use the information for your good.

So, this means that you must oversee your narrative, be aware that you are the only one who is going to affect a change in your life and that is what it means to take control. Before deliberating more about taking control, you should know that a conversation around taking back control could signify that a person has lost control previously.

Control over one's life is not always lost to another person; sometimes people lose control of themselves to an idea, their environment, or a vague concept that takes them off the disciplined path.

Regardless of what you relinquished control for, you must regain it now because it is required for the journey of self-discipline. Taking control of your life starts with the process of rediscovering what motivates you, learning how to take care of yourself, doing the things you love and making time for the people you care about. How are you going to do that?

Practice Having "Me" Time

From the beginning of the week until the last day of the month, some people are occupied with work, meetings and every other activity other than creating time for themselves.

They are always on the move, thinking about the next deal or idea to execute and even when they have some time that should be used for themselves, they look for something else to keep them busy.

To take control of your life, it is crucial that you have some "Me" time because it offers you an opportunity to stay in touch with your goals and aspirations while disconnecting from activities that clog your time.

The "Me" times you create, will give you a significant positive boost and energy required for the bigger goals you want to attain. If you cannot control your time, then it will be impossible for you to control your life.

Start taking charge of your life by first taking control of your time. Regardless of your obligations, "Me" time is essential and the more you implement it, the better your chances of taking control of your life. As you create time for yourself, you will also want to try new things.

Try New Things

This is one habit you will be grateful you developed. People who do not have control over their lives cannot try new things. They are always held down by the expectations of others or by other things they think they should be doing.

If you feel like your life is being run by activities and you aren't the one in charge, change the situation by trying new things you ordinarily wouldn't decide on your own. Break free from the constraints of sticking to familiar routines and events you are used to, come on! Life is all about being daring, and it does take a certain level of discipline to try new ventures.

You may not have to try new things every single day but do try them periodically. Step away from your comfort zone, live freely and enjoy every moment. What you will observe as you try this step is that you will be in better control of your life, you will be able to do the things you want to do while staying happy with yourself.

The Cure to Laziness (This Could Change Your Life)

Let's talk about happiness for a moment, shall we? When a person is in control of his/her life, the feeling of happiness is constant. You will always be satisfied with your life such that there are no insecurities nor internal problems.

What are the things you have always wanted to try out? Skydiving? Are you taking a trip to Africa? Or babysitting? Volunteering? Whatever you want to do, take control of your life and time.

As you build yourself up on this path to self-discipline, be comfortable with the idea of breaking the rules sometimes. Everyone will tell you to do the same thing repeatedly, but it is okay to get a breather and do something new.

Make this the year of saying "Yes" to new and positive adventures while exploring a wide range of options. Build up your experience bank with new memories, and you may ask "What if my love for trying out new things affects my plan for self-discipline?"

The answer to that question is encapsulated in one word: planning. The idea for you to try new things isn't to make you undisciplined. With careful consideration and planning, you can fit your entire schedule (including the new ideas) into your routine and make it work.

You will be able to handle everything you should be doing when you dedicate time to planning. However, open your heart to continuous learning through new things. Experiences gained by exploration of new ideas will always be of immense benefit to you.

As you try new things, something remarkable happens to you as well which also helps you take better control of your life. You will observe that you have become kinder to yourself which is one of the hallmarks of a disciplined person.

Treat Yourself Well as You Would Others

We are always quick to express kindness to others, society raises us to say the right things, to reach out to someone else and make them smile but what about being kind to self?

Some people who have tried being proactive about new things attest to the fact that it made them very kind to themselves. They no longer held themselves back from enjoying a treat or getting themselves a present because they are starting to be adventurous.

Well, a significant way for you to take charge of your life is to treat yourself the way you would treat others (positively of course). When you are deliberate about being kind to yourself, you will be taking control of what happens to you.

It is okay to expect kindness from other people especially when you are also kind as well, but when you feel bad because other people aren't helpful to you, you unknowingly give them control of your life.

The Cure to Laziness (This Could Change Your Life)

This is the year it ends; this is the season to take back control of your life and not allow anyone to get the best of your emotions. If there are certain dishes you only use to serve your guests, get them out and use them for your meal.

Say kind words to yourself every day, get yourself flowers and do all those nice things you would do for other people. Remember that you are on this pathway that promises great results, so you've got nothing to lose.

When other people do something, they're not proud of, they look to you for kind words, and you try to make them feel alright. But if you make a mistake on this journey to self-discipline, you become so hard on yourself. So, it seems like you set the bar too high for yourself and don't do the same for the people around you.

Give yourself a break by treating yourself with the same kind of respect you have for others and continually tell yourself you deserve the best. Now you are wondering how this connects to your self-discipline journey.

Well, only people who take control of their lives excel with self-discipline; treating yourself with kindness as you will treat others is an opportunity to oversee your life, and that helps you become a disciplined person.

Enjoy the Power of Saying "NO."

If you say "Yes" to all requests from everyone who asks, you will be losing control of your life. There is so much power in saying no because it helps you take back control. People don't want to say "No" because they don't want to feel guilty or hurt someone else, but can you make the entire world happy? If you always put the satisfaction of other people ahead of what you want, you will NOT be a self-disciplined person.

For example, if you decide to lose weight today, you might have to stay off some food or activities for a while. As you try to get rid of these items that make you struggle with weight loss, your friends may want to continue in the same unhealthy pattern.

So, they invite you over for parties where unhealthy foods are served, they don't want to exercise, they encourage your bad eating habits, and because you don't want them to feel bad or you don't want to be the boring one in the group, you give in to their suggestions every time.

The more you say "Yes" to them, the more control they assert over your life. Gradually, you will not remember your goals to lose weight, you will not be inspired to do the things that must be done, and you will no longer be motivated to do anything that makes you self-disciplined.

Control over your life is determined by the number of "No's" you say to requests that do not add value to your experience. You mustn't be a part of every event that takes place; selectivity is a trait disciplined people exhibit.

Realize that you own your time and only say yes to what adds value to it. The urge to please everyone stems from an undisciplined mindset; it is the fastest way to pulling down everything you've learned so don't allow it even for a moment.

Now self-discipline also comes to play here in another form; some people can say "No," but they cannot sustain it. So, they say "No," but if the person who is asking probes further with continuous requests and pleas, they say "Yes." This trait is referred to as being indecisive.

Indecisive people do not become disciplined; they struggle with the idea of pleasing themselves and other people that they become conflicted. Don't be an indecisive person! Be bold to make decisions and stick by them; by doing this, you will be taking control of your life and building up self-discipline as well.

What Is Life Teaching You?

Life is filled with lessons; if you are observant enough, you will never stop learning. Take control of your life by learning life-long lessons through the activities and events you experience daily.

We often try to resist life's lessons because they come in ways we don't expect, some lessons are in the form of mistakes, and because we are so consumed with the idea of being perfect, we miss the lesson embedded in the experience.

Embrace all that life teaches you, and you will know how to gain control over your own life. If you had a challenging experience, don't focus on the challenge itself or how it affects you. Try to figure out what you can learn from the problem.

The next time you are faced with a similar challenge, you will be able to handle it better because of the lesson you learned from the previous experience. However, this time you've gained control over your life; you will not be uncomfortable with the issue or distraught because life's lesson has strengthened you.

So, ask yourself right now; what is life teaching you? From everything that has happened to you, what have you learned? How have the experiences made you better? You will know when you are in control of life when experiences do not define your mood or attitude towards self-discipline.

With lessons from life, you can create an atmosphere of wisdom around you such that you always know what to do every time you are faced with a situation, and this is what being in control of one's life means.

A problem can pave the way for multiple solutions in your life, pay attention to what experiences are teaching you; you will be amazed

at how far you grow into becoming a self-disciplined person who in-
spires others to take the same path.

A person who has gained control over his/her life will enjoy the ben-
efits of self-discipline. Power makes independence possible; it helps
you do what you want to do when you should do it and encourages you
to continue the path you have created for yourself.

You become aware of the power you possess to cause changes and
rely on your strength for positive results. The absence of control
makes you susceptible to irregular activities; today you feel excited
about self-discipline by doing the right things, and the following day,
you are not so enthusiastic.

Unbalanced decisions do not blend with discipline, but you can correct
this pattern by being in charge. It's okay to take suggestions and ad-
vice, but if the people around you are not giving you the best advice,
then it is time to take control of your life.

- Do the things you want to do.

- Trust the process you create.

- Believe in your ability to win.

The above progressions are just some of the ways you can take con-
trol of your life. Tell yourself these truths every day, and you will be
able to combat the feeling of losing control. Your life can be fun,

progressive and inspiring; what you need to do is TAKE CHARGE! Own your truth and don't stop building yourself on the path to self-discipline.

Conclusion

Self-discipline is an attainable virtue anyone can imbibe especially when the individual has a manual to follow. There is a process for everything that can be achieved in life and what you have received from this book is a definitive guide containing the significant aspects you can work on consistently until you reach your desired goal.

The fact that you are reading a book on self-discipline shows how committed you are to the process but is process enough? Can a person become self-disciplined just by sticking to a method?

It's akin to having a reading timetable for an upcoming examination. While having a schedule is brilliant, does having it alone guarantee a pass at the exam? As mentioned in a previous chapter, being process-oriented isn't enough, you've got to go beyond adopting the process and be more conscious of the protocol it entails.

By protocol, we mean the rules of conduct and behavior to imbibe for a wish to become a reality. Without a procedure, the process will not be enough. As you implement everything you've learned with this material, remember that the purpose of it all is to help you establish a protocol that makes the process a part of your daily reality.

So, with forming new habits, for example, you shouldn't be fixated on just "How" to create the pattern. You should however become more conscious about the activities you can do every day that will strengthen the newly formulated habit.

Your ability to maintain the lessons learned in the sections of this book will determine how impactful your experience will be. This will ultimately introduce the concept of sustainability in life.

The internet is replete with information about how everyone can become better with self-discipline yet, millions of people still struggle with the idea of taking charge of their own lives. One can only wonder why this is a case, with so much knowledge out there.

Well, the reason for the above assertion is a lack of sustaining power; too many people read, but only a few implements what they discover. For you to create a connection between theories and results, you must become passionate about sustainability.

Having good habits, building a positive mindset, taking control of your life and every other idea you gleaned from this book can become a vital part of your life long-term if you are deliberate about sustaining them.

This means you are going to apply the concepts every day (regardless of how the results trickle in). And while using them, remember that the process is just a means to an end, what matters the most is the pattern you establish which is also known as the "Protocol".

Nothing can successfully stand in the way of a person who is determined to become self-disciplined. Through this book, you have gained access to applicable patterns that will provide useful results that take you from where you are now to where you want to be. What are you waiting for to get started?

If you find this book helpful in anyway a review to support my endeavors is much appreciated.

Stephen Martin

The Cure to Laziness (This Could Change Your Life)